DOROTHY HAMILL
ON AND OFF THE ICE

DOROTHY HAMILL

On and Off the Ice

BY DOROTHY HAMILL
With Elva Clairmont

ALFRED A. KNOPF, NEW YORK

For Jonsie, Bill, Mom, Dad,
Marcia, Sandy, and Dean,
who have surrounded me with their
love and support

<hr />

THIS IS A BORZOI BOOK PUBLISHED BY ALFRED A. KNOPF, INC.

Text copyright © 1983 by Dorothy Hamill
Front-of-jacket photograph copyright © 1983 by Barbara Bordnick
Back-of-jacket photograph copyright © 1981 by Jerry Wachter
All rights reserved under International and Pan-American Copyright Conventions. Published in the United States by Alfred A. Knopf, Inc., New York, and simultaneously in Canada by Random House of Canada Limited, Toronto. Distributed by Random House, Inc., New York.
Manufactured in the United States of America.

Library of Congress Cataloging in Publication Data. Hamill, Dorothy. Dorothy Hamill on and off the ice. Summary: The author describes her life and evolution into one of the world's most famous ice skaters. 1. Hamill, Dorothy. 2. Skaters—United States—Biography. [1. Hamill, Dorothy. 2. Ice skaters] I. Clairmont, Elva. II. Title.
GV850.H3A37   1983   796.91'092'4   [B]   [92]   83-6170
ISBN 0-394-85610-4   ISBN 0-394-95610-9 (lib. bdg.)

Picture Credits appear on page 182
Book design by Mina Greenstein. Calligraphy by Edward Diehl.
FIRST EDITION

2   4   6   8   10   9   7   5   3   1

Acknowledgments

So many people have contributed in so many ways to my journey towards the Olympic gold medal, and have continued to support me and believe in me since I turned professional, that it is impossible to thank them all by name. They know who they are and I want to assure them that their contributions—every word of encouragement and every helping hand—will never be forgotten. There are, however, a few special people that I feel compelled to single out because their love and encouragement has been instrumental in the shaping of my life. In no particular order, I would like to thank:

Michael Rosenberg, for helping me to chart the course of my career;

Nancy Pond, for always being there when I needed her;

The late Edwin Mosler and Mr. and Mrs. Pete Hoyt, for their generous financial support;

Mrs. Ellen Long, the Streeter family and Dr. and Mrs. Henry Landis, for sharing their homes and their families with me;

The Danks family—especially Kim—for understanding that friendship lives in the heart;

My agent, Elliott Kozak and my publicist, Janice Burenga, for their tireless attention;

Bob Allen, the manager of the Olympic Arena in Lake Placid, who was always there when it counted, rooting for me;

Mrs. Siatka, who sewed such wonderful costumes, including my Olympic costume;

Suga, who is not just a hair stylist, but an angel who changed my life;

Mort West, who has always taken such very good care of me;

Doug Wilson and ABC's Wide World of Sports team, who have all done so much for skating over the years and have helped me so often in my own career;

The Ice Capades—that happiest of families—especially George and Denise Eby and Dick and Rita Palmer, for their generous and continued support and encouragement; Don Watson, Bob Gallagher and Chuck Walters, company managers for Capades, who took care of me on the road; and David Doucette, a marvelous costume designer, who designed my wedding dress;

Ricci and Gina, good friends as well as in-laws, who have brought me such warmth and laughter;

Dean Martin—Dad—whom I adore, and who still thinks I am the girl who throws chewing gum into the pool;

Jeannie, my mother-in-law, who is the most together lady I have ever met in my life. I want to thank her for making me feel like I belong in her family;

Desi Arnaz, Jr.—thank God for Desi in so many ways, but most of all for bringing Dean into my life;

MY OWN FAMILY—

Mom and Dad, for giving up so much for so long and for still being there at the other end;

My beloved sister and brother, Marcia and Sandy, who made sacrifices in their own ways, but never resented me;

Jonsie and Bill, who taught me so much about love and who will always be with me in my heart;

Gammy—Grandmother Hamill—who was a wonderful, strong lady and who I remember with deep affection;

Perky and Bucky, for making my brother and my sister so happy; and Bronwyn and Whitney, my nieces;

The De Lio family for all their guidance and help in Colorado and for keeping my skates sharp!

All the men at G. Stanzione's for making my boots over the years;

Frank Brill, for really caring;

The Colorado Academy, a school that understands the true meaning of education and gave me back my love of learning;

Andy Warhol, for sharing with me his sense of individuality;

The two Kathy's—McVey and Porter—both of whom, in their own distinct ways, have been such fine friends to me;

Karen Carpenter, who was always there at the right time—I miss her;

Dwight Hemion, Gary Smith and Rob Iscove, for sharing their unique talents in the world of television;

The town of Greenwich, Connecticut, and the Rye Figure Skating Club, for their constant and generous support;

The blind and handicapped children all over the world, some of whom I have been fortunate enough to meet, whose love and courage is an inspiration to us all;

Barbara Taplan, whose tragic death this year has left me with a sense of loss;

Gustave Lussi, whose sure hand has guided so many free skaters over the years—so much of what I am is Gus, and I am forever indebted to him for the courage he gave me out on the ice;

Ellen Burka and Brian Foley, for all their inspiration, their talents and their constant belief in me;

Sonya and Peter Dunfield, who brought me through so many crises and delivered me intact;

Peter Burrows, who was there when I needed him most, right before the Olympic Games, and who so often helped me with a kind word or a caring gesture;

Carlo and Christa Fassi, for bringing me into their home and providing a path to the top;

Harold Nicholson, who, although he is not mentioned in this book, did spend many patient hours watching my circles;

JoJo Starbuck and her mother, Alice, for all the years of fun and love;

Gordie McKellen, Robin Cousins and Brian Pockar, each of whom in his own way has enriched my life;

And—finally—all those skaters everywhere who have improved and developed the sport and the art of figure skating, many of whom have never received recognition for their work; I especially single out John Curry—who for me represents the skater's skater. He taught me that it is not only possible, but also imperative, for a great skater to be both artist and athlete. I want him to know that I am still working at it, and that his endless caring and love for skaters everywhere, no matter what their rank, is something I very much admire.

For their help with this book, I would like to thank my editor, Frances Foster, and all the wonderful staff at Knopf, including Laura Woodworth, Colleen Brennan, Katherine Banks, Denise Cronin, Mina Greenstein, Mimi Harrison, Steve Bloom and Wendy Hashmall.

Looking back over the years portrayed in this book has been an emotional experience for me. I have been forced to examine the results of a career that has already spanned sixteen years, and in doing so I have come to the conclusion that—although I have been fortunate enough to have achieved much already—I am far from satisfied. I am not yet ready to hang up my skates.

To me the future has always stretched ahead of me in a warm, enticing arc—like a rainbow waiting to be climbed. I can't see the other end, but that doesn't matter. The important thing is the journey. It has to be the important thing, because the truth is that rainbows have no end.

Contents

Some years ago, when I was almost eleven, a famous Canadian skater came down to the rink in Lake Placid where I was training for the summer. He stopped to watch me skate, following every movement with great concentration. When I saw who it was I rushed to get my autograph book and add his signature to my rapidly growing collection of names. He held the book for a moment, looked at me shrewdly, and wrote:

To Dear Dorothy
I'm sure you will be great one day.
Toller Cranston.

DOROTHY HAMILL
ON AND OFF THE ICE

ONE

The End of the Beginning

*T*HE night I won the Olympics everyone urged me to stop competing. To quit. I was told I had nothing further to gain—I was the new Ladies' Olympic Champion. I had won the highest honor skating has to offer and had established a reputation that would only be put at risk by entering the World Figure Skating Championship in Göteborg, Sweden, three weeks later. I should retire from amateur competition while I was still ahead.

But it wasn't that simple. Something inside me wasn't satisfied—not yet. I had never won a World Championship, and in the eyes of the skating world that was the final test. I knew that if I gave up now, without trying this one last time, I would regret it for the rest of my life.

The telephone never stopped ringing. Thousands of telegrams and flowers poured into my hotel room from fans all over the world. I received staggering offers from potential managers and agents, producers and promoters. Barbara Streisand telephoned in the middle of the night to recommend her manager to us. It was a little like being on a merry-go-round which wouldn't stop. It was exhilarating, exhausting and—in the end—it overwhelmed me. I shut it out.

The Olympic Gold! With silver-medalist
Dianne Deleeuw, left, and bronze-medalist
Christine Errath, right

Carlo Fassi, my trainer, was among those who were against my going on. "You have so much to lose, Dorothy," he said. "You are the Olympic Champion. It is enough."

I was shocked. Didn't he believe that I would win the Worlds? Why else would he oppose my entering it? Did he think that my Olympic win had been a fluke? Suddenly I knew that I was going to have to prove myself even to him.

My dad went back to Connecticut to deal with the chaos that followed my Olympic victory. Our house and garden were filled with parcels, flowers and letters from well-wishers. The answering service had been forced to put on extra staff to deal with the deluge of phone calls. Dad's plan was to reduce this confusion to a manageable situation, ready for the time I arrived home— whether that was in the immediate future or after the Worlds.

In the meantime Mom took me to Vienna. She knew how much I had always loved that romantic city and felt it would soothe me and help me to reach a decision. She stayed by my side as she had done all through my long years of skating, supporting me quietly, giving me time to make up my own mind. She knew that this was a decision only I could make.

We left Vienna and took the train to Munich. From there we were either going to fly to Helsinki, where I would go back into training for the Worlds, or fly home. As we rattled through the German countryside, I stared out the window at the snow. My mother sat beside me, knitting patiently, not disturbing my thoughts. I thought about all the glamorous things I had been offered in the last few days—the millions of dollars I had been promised. At nineteen I was about to enter a tantalizing world where I would be the star of an ice show. After all the long years of hard work as an amateur, forbidden to accept anything more than expense money as payment for skating, I was on the verge of wealth and fame. I had the chance to pay back my parents for all the sacrifices they had made for me over the years. But I decided it would all have to wait a bit longer. I had unfinished business to attend to. When the train drew into the Munich station, I knew what I was going to do. I was going on.

Training in Helsinki was hard. I had to get my body back into shape again. I hadn't skated since the Olympics, and at the height of competition even a week off the ice can make a great deal of difference. I also had to make sure my mental attitude was right; that is at least as important as good physical conditioning. I put everything out of my mind—all the offers, the phone calls, the talk of shows and television specials. I thought only of skating and the approaching competitions in Sweden. The Olympics seemed a lifetime ago.

TWO WEEKS later I arrived in Göteborg. It was covered with ice and snow. As I looked for familiar faces I realized many were missing. Skaters had quit, not wanting to subject themselves to the further strain of the World Championship. I felt a peculiar sense of loss.

Then on the morning of the Ladies' school figures I saw John Curry. Like me, he had won an Olympic gold medal in Innsbruck and had trained with Carlo Fassi. John had never won a World Championship either, so had faced the same dilemma of choosing whether or not to continue. When I didn't see him in Helsinki, I assumed he had quit. I skated over to the barriers where he was standing and he leaned over and hugged me. "I came to give you some support," he said. Then he smiled. "I hope you'll do the same for me." I was so thrilled that John had decided to try again. He told me he didn't know how well he would do because he hadn't been on the ice since the Olympics.

In the end he did extremely well. He won his first World

The winning program at the Worlds, Göteborg, 1976

Championship and established himself once and for all as a great champion. Now it was my turn.

I had no doubts going into that Championship. I felt almost fatalistic about it, as though it were out of my hands. I had done everything I could to prepare for it and now all there was to do was skate.

I stood on the ice waiting to start the final phase of the

Championship—the free skating. I was in first place after school figures and the compulsory short program. I knew I had a very good chance for the gold medal. I saw Carlo pacing nervously at the entrance to the ice; I saw John Curry, his own test already over, offering me his strength and support; and I saw my dad standing there patiently, willing me to make it through this one last battle. He knew, more than anyone else, what it meant to me. I thought of Mom, who couldn't bear to watch me go through it all again. She was pacing nervously, chain-smoking back in her hotel room.

Then the music began and I started to skate. For the next four minutes I forgot everything except the steps, the spins, the jumps. I moved across the great ice surface, carried along on a tide of emotion. This was to be the last time—the final test. No matter what happened, I would never compete again. I wanted to make this one count.

As I came off the ice at the end of the performance, I saw people standing. I heard the cheering and saw American flags waving in the air. John hugged me tightly. Carlo lumbered up and pumped my hand. My dad came running down the steps and I knew from the look on his face that I had done it. I was finally the World Champion.

As I stood on the winner's podium, listening to the "Star Spangled Banner," I felt a lump in my throat and tears in my eyes. In some ways this victory meant more to me than any other. I had won the Olympics for my country—for all those Americans whose love and good wishes carried me through those last few days in Innsbruck. But I had won the World Championship for myself, and for all those people who had believed in me and helped me since I first put on skates down by Morse's Pond.

9 years old, 1965

Lucking Out

*T*HE first time I can remember skating was on Morse's Pond behind my grandparents' house in Wellesley, Massachussetts. I must have been about eight years old and I wore a battered old pair of family skates that had belonged first to my brother Sandy and then to my sister Marcia. They were too big for me but my grandmother padded them with foam rubber to make them fit. I sat on the bank of the pond trying to lace the boots with impatient, frozen fingers. At last I struggled upright, wobbling precariously. I took a cautious step forward and, as I felt the ice under my blades, something inside me surged.

I skated many times that winter. We lived in Riverside, Connecticut, close enough to my grandparents that Marcia and I could visit them often. The first thing I did on arrival at their house was to make sure the ice was still solid. I grew to love gliding slowly across the hard peppermint-colored surface of the pond. I would see my grandmother watching me from her kitchen window, and when I was absolutely shaking with cold I would rush into the house and let her rub my feet with a warm bath towel. Then she would give me a cup of steaming coffee laced heavily with sugar and real cream. Since my mother didn't allow us to have coffee, I never told her about it. Grandmother said it was good for me—the sugar would give me energy and the cream would give me calcium for my bones. "If you're going to skate," she told me, "you have to make sure your bones are strong. Otherwise, they'll break." I agreed with her, not because I knew anything about calcium, but because I always agreed with my grandmother.

Grandmother's maiden name was Esther Jones and we called her Jonsie. When I was a baby she had been in a bad car accident which left her with a pinched nerve in her spinal cord. She wore a neck brace and part of her face was paralyzed, but to me she was the most beautiful woman on earth. She was very tall, like my mother, and she was athletic and strong in spite of the accident.

Grandfather's name was Willis Clough. We all called him Bill. He was a Harvard graduate, tall, handsome and very elegant. Until he retired he worked for the Sheraton Hotel chain, furnishing the presidential and corporate suites in all the new hotels. He traveled around the world buying fine furniture and art work, and brought Jonsie the most beautiful antique perfume bottles from London and Paris. I loved to sit by the fire in the evenings listening to Bill's stories about his travels. He met Jonsie while he was still at Harvard. She was a dental hygenist, and one day while she was cleaning his teeth she promised to give it all up and marry him. It was a good choice because they were the greatest friends all their lives. I don't think either one of them ever spoke a cross word.

ONE DAY, back home in Riverside, I spotted a pair of skates in Caldor's Department Store. They were the most beautiful things I had ever seen—white with bright red trim. I ran to get my mother and asked her to let me try them on. They fit

Jonsie and Bill

perfectly. She admired them and asked how much they cost. When she heard they were five dollars she shook her head. "Maybe next Christmas," she said. I went home crushed. I had never really asked for anything in my life, but I knew I had to have those skates. I begged my mother twenty times a day. I went to my father who told me to ask my mother. I tried enlisting the support of my brother, but at the superior age of twelve he had no time for my problems. I had almost given up when one day I came home from school and found a box on the kitchen table. My mother smiled and pushed the box toward me. "Since these seemed to mean so much to you," she said, "we thought you'd better have them."

Inside the box, nestled in a bed of white tissue, were the skates. At last I had skates of my own—skates that fit me. Marcia and her friend let me go with them to the pond near our house. I was very excited. As I glided out onto the ice my new skates felt wonderful. I made my way slowly around the edge and looked behind me for the others. They were approaching at a great speed, skating not forward but backwards. As they passed they gave me a triumphant look. Not to be left out, I tried to turn around so that I, too, could skate backwards. But I lost control of my legs and fell down. Again and again I tried. I begged Marcia to show me how but she was too busy with her friend. Finally I was so bruised from falling and so frustrated that I went home in tears.

Seeing how upset I was at not being able to skate backwards and realizing how determined I was to learn, my mother enrolled me in a series of eight group lessons. I went once a week after school to an ice rink in Rye, New York. We learned only the most elementary moves, but to my delight skating backwards was one of them. In the last week of lessons I learned how to do a mohawk. I didn't realize it then but this simplest of moves— turning from a forward skating position to a backward position—is the first step towards competitive skating.

I was eager to learn more and Mom enrolled me in a summer class at Shirley Ayre's Ice Studio in the Stamford Shopping Mall. The first day the teacher looked at my skates, felt the ankles and told my mother they just wouldn't do. "There's no support," she said. "She could injure herself wearing these."

That weekend we went to visit Jonsie and told her about the skates. Her answer was to put on her hat and coat and take us

Early publicity shots

Marcia, Sandy, and me, 1959

to a large Sears Roebuck store in Framingham. In the sporting goods department we found a pair of good, firm skates that fitted me well. They cost twelve-fifty reduced from fifteen dollars, which was more than my mother had in mind to pay. Jonsie, however, talked her into it. "After all," she reasoned, "how can you afford to turn them down? You'll be saving two-fifty."

I returned to my lessons properly equipped and began to learn a new kind of mohawk—this time counter-clockwise.

THAT SUMMER of 1965 I turned nine and learned to swim. I wanted to compete in the races at the Riverside Yacht Club but the meets were held on Wednesday mornings, the same time as my skating lessons. Obviously I couldn't do both. My friends kept urging me to come swimming and finally I asked my mother if I could give up skating.

She listened to me and then shook her head. "You asked me to pay for skating lessons and I paid for them," she said. "You needed new skates and I bought them. I made a commitment to you. Your commitment to me was to go to the lessons and learn to skate. I have honored my commitment and now you must honor yours." The subject was closed.

As my skating improved my enthusiasm grew. By the end of the lessons I was able to do a bunny hop—the easiest of all the jumps. For this feat—hopping into the air while skating forward—I was awarded a prize of a free half-hour private lesson.

The lesson came and went all too quickly. Afterwards my teacher encouraged my mother to sign me up for a series of lessons. "Your daughter shows signs of real talent," she said.

My mother read the look on my face and smiled. "I might as well save myself the weeks of pleading and say yes now."

So I was signed up for a weekly private lesson with Barbara Taplan, and we had picked a very talented teacher by sheer accident. One of her students had become a National Champion. It is very important to establish good habits in the early stages of skating and, fortunately for me, the technique Barbara taught me in that first year was an excellent underpinning for my years of free skating. I had lucked out.

Later that summer we all went to stay with my grandparents in their summer home in Rockport, Massachusetts, an old fishing village on the Atlantic, north of Boston. Vacations there were always the highlight of the year. Long ago my grandfather bought twelve acres of beachfront property and built a home on it. Then he built a guest house because, although he liked to entertain, he also liked his privacy. In the evening we would go down to the docks to watch the fishing boats come in and to buy fresh fish or lobster for dinner. During the day we would pick buckets of fresh blueberries which grew in abundance on my grandparents' land. Jonsie would bake blueberry muffins, pancakes and pies. I can still remember the smell of the air in Rockport—it was soft and sweet, filled with the scent of pines. Often in the evening, I would walk down to the edge of the sea and sit on the rocks. I stared very hard at the horizon, trying to see the coast of England. Like my own future, I knew it was there, but I just couldn't make out its shape.

Marcia and me with
Mom and Dad, 1964

THREE

Initiation

*I*N the fall of that year I began the weekly private lessons with Barbara Taplan. She taught in Rye, New York, in an amusement park called Playland.

I was an impatient student, wanting to go flying around the ice, spinning and jumping, but Barbara insisted I move forward slowly. She would make me go over and over moves I felt were already perfect. "You have to get it right," she said. "There's no point in going on to something new unless you've mastered the last thing." She knew that without solid preparation figure skating can be very dangerous, so we advanced through the fall at a snail's pace, building a solid technical base.

One day a lady at the rink told my mom about the Wollman Open, a competition held each year on the outdoor Wollman Rink in New York City's Central Park. She told my mother I should enter. My mother protested that I was only nine years old but the lady insisted it made no difference. It would be good experience for me. The seed was sown.

A month later my dad drove me down to New York City with my skates in the back of the car and my entry slip in my hand. When we arrived at the rink there were about a hundred little

Wollman Rink, New York City, 1966

girls milling around on the ice. As I watched them all warming up I suddenly became very nervous. I saw girls doing axel jumps— one-and-a-half revolutions in the air—a very difficult jump which I was far from ready to tackle. What I didn't know was that I was watching most of the top Juvenile skaters from the eastern United States.

My dad was very calm about it and told me to go out there and just enjoy myself. "Don't even think about competing," he said. "Just have fun."

I relaxed once I felt the ice under my blades. Barbara had helped me to make up my program which was not very difficult technically but used every beat of the music well. It included a bell jump, clapping the feet together in the air, and a waltz jump which is the first jump most skaters learn—a half-revolution in the air.

When I finished I waited around for the results. I felt awkward because all the other kids seemed to know each other. I was an outsider. When the results were posted I couldn't get near the list because of the crowd around it. All the kids were screaming and jumping up and down. Suddenly they stopped and turned to look at me. "You were second," someone said accusingly, and they all stared. I felt my head float away from my body, I was so happy. I couldn't believe it.

On the way back to Connecticut my dad began to show an interest in my skating. Until then he had not been aware of how important it was becoming to me. When we got home he took out a clean notebook and headed it "Dorothy—Skating." And he filled in the date and the details of the Wollman Open.

My dad is a very distinguished looking man. He is about five feet eight inches tall and has iron gray hair and pronounced jowls. He was one of seven children and perhaps because of the confusion that reigned in so large a family, he has an obsession with orderliness. He keeps a record of everything that happens to us—every medal, every flu shot, every grade is recorded meticulously in a series of notebooks. Now he was going to keep a record of my skating career and, as he filled in the details of that first competition, he had no idea how many notebooks it would eventually involve.

By SPRING most of the winter facilities had closed for the season and we couldn't find any ice for me to practice on. Barbara had gone to teach on Long Island, which was too far for me to travel. One day we discovered, quite by accident, the Crystal Ice Palace in Norwalk, Connecticut, and I started going there several times a week. I made friends with a girl named Missy. The rink was old and dilapidated and the ice was a series of hills and valleys, but we quickly learned how to cope.

One afternoon I saw Missy down at the far end of the rink with some other girls, taking a class from a small man who resembled a bear. He was dressed in an enormous fluffy overcoat and he strode up and down in front of his class like a ringmaster. I watched for a few minutes and then turned to my mother.

"I wish I could take lessons from that man with Missy," I said.

When he had finished teaching, Mom asked him if I could join his class, and he said he'd be glad to have me. His name was Otto Gold and we found out later that he was one of the world's foremost skating teachers. He was Czechoslovakian and as a young man had been a European skating champion. He was a strict disciplinarian and insisted I change some of the style Barbara had taught me. His methods, he told us, were to be strictly adhered to at all times. He had an explosive temper if something upset him, but he would be just as quick to let out a huge, deep laugh if something amused him. To tell the truth, I was a little afraid of Mr. Gold.

My skating improved rapidly under his eagle eye. He began to teach me school figures, which are the equivalent of scales to a pianist. They are the underlying technique upon which all other skating is based. One afternoon he asked my mother why I didn't belong to the Southern Connecticut Figure Skating Club. "That way she could take her figure skating tests," he said.

My mother looked blank. "What are those?" she asked.

He explained that skaters took a series of tests to establish their level of competence. These tests are administered under the strictest conditions in a registered skating club and governed by the rules of the United States Figure Skating Association (U.S.F.S.A.). The first test is the Preliminary and this is followed by eight more. Skaters who have passed their Eighth Test (or Gold Test) are qualified to compete in Senior competitions. My mother decided I might as well give it a try.

The headquarters of the Southern Connecticut Ice Skating Club were right there at the Crystal Ice Palace, and that spring I took the Preliminary Test. Mr. Gold's wife helped my mother make me a dress for the test. It was made of blue bonded flannel and came down to my knees. When we arrived at the rink, Mr. Gold took one look and shook his head.

"Too long," he told Mother.

So my mom pinned and sewed right up till it was time for me to skate, and I was so proud of my new thigh-length dress that I forgot to be nervous. The test consisted of seven figures, four of which were simple stroking exercises to gauge the skater's ability to hold a clean edge and use correct push-offs when changing feet. The other three were variations of a figure eight— two circle eights and a waltz eight. The judges were looking for steadiness and a bent, flexible knee. I seemed to satisfy them on both counts because I passed and was allowed to move on to the First Test.

I missed Barbara Taplan's warm, gentle humor and motherly encouragement. But there was no doubt that I was making progress with Mr. Gold. When school was out he invited me to Lake Placid to train with him during the summer. He told my parents I could live with him and his wife and take daily skating lessons. To my delight they agreed, and we began to make preparations. I was to leave in three weeks.

My whole life now seemed to be centered around ice. My best friend Kim, who had been my constant companion until this year, barely saw me any more. We talked about the skating and the demands it made on my time and she insisted that she understood. She said it made no difference at all to our friendship. But I missed her—I missed the games we used to play and the long, heart-to-heart conversations we shared after school and on weekends. I felt a wall closing around me and experienced my first taste of the essential loneliness of a life dominated by a single goal. I wondered fleetingly if this was what I really wanted, but I already knew the answer. I was into skating for the long haul, no matter what the cost, no matter where it took me. I already knew it was worth it.

LAKE PLACID, in the Adirondack Mountains of northern New York State, is one of the great winter sports capitals of the world. The Winter Olympics was held there in 1932 and again in 1980. It has also become, over the years, a very important summer training center for skaters, and I was excited as we drove up to Mr. Gold's house in the center of the village. My parents had coffee with the Golds and then they kissed me goodbye and left. As I watched their car disappear from sight around a bend in the road I swallowed hard. I wasn't sure that I was going to be able to keep from crying. I had never been away from home on my own before.

Gradually, however, I got over my homesickness. Mr. Gold worked us very hard and we put in far more hours than I had ever worked on ice before. Each night I would drag myself home exhausted, but in some strange way, exhilarated. I was learning so much—my figures were improving rapidly.

I was in love with Gordie McKellen who was later to become a United States Champion. I was not alone because all the little girls in Lake Placid that summer were in love with Gordie. He is the godson of the great ice champion, Sonja Henie, and the son of the great ice comedian, Tuffy McKellen. Gordie had blue eyes and curly hair and a marvelous sense of humor. He was fourteen that summer of 1966 and sometimes he would come to the rink and help us kids. He told us we were very lucky to be working with Mr. Gold—the man who had trained the 1948 Olympic Champion, Barbara Ann Scott.

I turned ten that July and passed my first figure test. It consisted of three circle eights and a three (all of which are variations on the basic figure eight), and two serpentines, which are made up of three circles joined together in a straight line. Two weeks later I passed the Second Test which required a circle eight, four threes and two serpentines. The edges and foot changes required were more difficult and complicated than those of the First Test. Each test is designed to demonstrate a greater control, flexibility and mastery of skating technique.

The big Lake Placid exhibition was held in August, and for a week beforehand all the great skating champions were arriving. They practiced at the rink and I watched them in awe. Was it possible that one day I would be able to skate like them? The gap between us seemed so big. I watched carefully as Peggy Fleming, the long-legged girl who had just won the World Championship in Davos, Switzerland, spun and jumped and seemed to float across the ice. She was magic. But it was not Peggy I wanted to skate like—it was the men I wanted to emulate. John Misha Petkevich was my idol. He was the first of a new breed of artistic skaters. I would watch him intently, trying to analyze his style. I watched all the champions—Tim Wood, Gary Visconti, Emmerich Danzer—by the hour. It was an unbelievable opportunity for a young skater.

In the middle of August Mr. Gold told us that we would all compete in a free skating competition at the end of the month. We were expected to work very hard to get ready for it. I was excited as it was my first opportunity to compete since the Wollman Open back in the winter. I felt confident that I could do much better this time. I wrote my dad and asked him to send me some music tapes for my program. When they came, I eagerly set about trying to choreograph my number. I had no idea how to begin or what to do, but I figured it couldn't be all that difficult.

The first tape was Herb Albert's "Java," the biggest hit tune of the summer. I spent four days frantically trying to skate to it, but it beat me. It was too fast and too tricky; I didn't have the technique for it. The other tape was a favorite of mine, "It's a Grand Night for Singing." Since this was my only remaining choice, I had to make this one work. I tried everything but just couldn't make the steps fit the beat of the music. In the end I gave up and decided to ad lib on the night of the competition.

My free skating was still very elementary—certainly not at the level required to ad lib. I gave a performance where I seemed to be fighting the music rather than skating to it. Under the

23

circumstances the judges were very kind. They awarded me eighth place. Even though I knew it was better than I deserved, I was disappointed.

My next competition was later that same week. One of my friends that summer was Cynthia Van Valkenburg, a girl who later became a very good pairs skater. She came flying across the rink to tell me there was to be a similar pairs event. "What's that?" I asked. "For two girls or two boys," she answered. "It's perfect for us. We're both ten and we're the same size exactly."

Indeed we were. As Jonsie would have said, we were both knee high to a grasshopper.

Cynthia had some music picked out and we went to tell Mr. Gold of our inspiration. He dismissed us with a shake of his head. "You are much too young—too inexperienced."

We crept away, determined to prove him wrong, and started to work on our routine. We felt that this was our big chance to make the skating world sit up and take notice of us. Friday arrived and—to Mr. Gold's horror—the Hamill-Van Valkenburg team made its debut. We were not a success. There was nothing the least bit similar about our similar pair, and since we both forgot the choreography after the first few beats we spent the remainder of the three minutes trying to catch up with one another. Crushed, we retired to the side of the rink, trying to avoid Mr. Gold's furious glare, and watched the other entrants. They were all Seniors who had been preparing their programs for weeks.

I wrote to Jonsie that night to tell her about the free skating competition. "I didn't do so well in the Juvenile Ladies'," I wrote. "I finished eighth. But I was fourth in similar pairs." What I didn't tell her was that there were only four entries.

My parents held a post-mortem with Mr. Gold after my disastrous showing in the Lake Placid competition. He told them that I was a very competent technical skater for my age but that I needed more experience and training in free skating. I needed to be taught how to enter and exit from technical elements gracefully and how to join free skating moves together. As I listened to this conversation I got the idea that I had an inborn lack of grace. It was a notion that was to stay with me for many years.

Convinced that I was a skater who could not handle artistic programs, I began to attack my skating ferociously: if I could not be artistic, then I would be athletic. I would jump higher and spin faster than any girl alive. I would even jump higher than Gordie McKellen. I was determined to prove myself the equal of any man on the ice. I even remember asking my dad if it was possible for me to enter the Men's category next time.

1966

FOUR

Endless Circles

*A*FTER that summer, Otto Gold moved back to Canada and I went back to training with Barbara Taplan. I was overjoyed. She was like a second mother to me, always warm and encouraging, and she made me feel secure about my skating in a way no one else could. The North Atlantic Championships were to be held in Lake Placid in the late fall and I made up my mind to enter the Juvenile division.

The Juvenile level is only the first of many levels on the way to international competition. After Juvenile comes the Intermediate level, then Novice, Junior and Senior. For Juvenile and Intermediate skaters, there are only local competitions. At the Novice, Junior and Senior levels, skaters who place in the top three in the local (or Regional) competitions move on to compete in the Sectionals; and the top skaters from the Sectionals go on to take part in the Nationals. The top skaters are drawn from four categories: Ladies' (my event), Men's, Pairs, and Ice Dance. The medalists from the Nationals each year make up the team sent to represent the United States in the World Championships, but in 1966 I knew little about international skating. I was far more concerned with my first Regional competition—the North Atlantics in Lake Placid.

Spreadeagle at the
Showboat Restaurant, 1967

My parents couldn't go with me so I went with Barbara and another one of her students. I wasn't the least bit nervous; in fact I was rather looking forward to it.

The Men's and Ladies' competitions had two phases. School figures came first and counted for fifty percent of the total mark. I placed sixth in school figures at the North Atlantics. Barbara was pleased and I was thrilled—but for a different reason. My mother had spent the previous week making me a new free skating costume. It was a deep turquoise blue and was the prettiest dress I had ever had. Only the first eight girls in school figures got to advance to the free skating phase, so by placing sixth I had assured myself of the opportunity to wear the new dress.

I went out to skate my free program confident that I could at least hold my own against the other girls. Barbara had been careful not to let me see them at practice, so I had no idea that most of them already could do several double jumps. I was still getting by with only two—a double salchow (named after the World Champion Ulrich Salchow and consisting of two complete turns in the air off a back inside edge) and a double toe loop (two turns in the air taking off from a slightly curved edge and using the toepick of the left foot to assist the takeoff). By this time I also had a consistent axel jump. But although I skated well that day and managed to land all my jumps cleanly, I had no idea just how far away I was from being fully competitive with the other Juvenile girls.

The audience applauded enthusiastically as I finished my program, and as I came off the ice Barbara gave me a big hug and told me she was proud of me. I was excited. I waited impatiently for the competition to end and for the marks to be posted up on the wall. I felt certain that this time I had done well.

However, my hopes were dashed when I saw my marks. They were very low and my disappointment showed on my face. Barbara leaned over and said, "Whatever you do, hold your head up and smile. Don't let them see you cry. You must accept whatever comes."

I fought to keep back the tears, but as soon as I reached the dressing room they came spilling out. I was crushed—I had skated as well as I could but still dropped to eighth place. I didn't understand then the basis on which the judges make their decisions. Even though I had skated well and executed my jumps and spins cleanly, my program lacked difficult technical moves. Barbara tried to explain it to me but I was not to be consoled. I was angry—not with the judges, because at the age of ten it didn't occur to me to question them—but with myself. I figured I just hadn't worked hard enough.

I went home to Connecticut very discouraged. For once in my life I was unable to eat. I moped around the house and as the days wore on, I grew more and more determined: there had to be a way—somehow I would become as good as those other serious skaters. It was a turning point in my life. I made a commitment to myself and from that moment on there was no turning back. I was going to have to work harder than I had ever worked before.

My parents realized that this was no ordinary disappointment. They went to see Barbara to discuss the situation. Her advice was simple. "Dorothy needs more skating time," she said. "She has to have more lessons, more focused concentration." She hesitated before going on. "It's going to mean a tremendous sacrifice not only for Dorothy, but also for the family. It's going to be expensive."

Mom had only one other question. "Do you really believe Dorothy has the talent it takes?" she asked.

29

Barbara looked at them steadily. "Yes," she said. "I know she has."

And so we entered a new phase. I began to take a lesson a day, five days a week. I got up before dawn to skate patch sessions—patch is named for the section of ice you are allotted to practice the all-important school figures. These school figures can make or break you at a championship and there is no other way to learn them than to spend hour after hour tracing and retracing the figures. There were mornings when I found the endless repetition boring beyond belief but it never occurred to me to stop. My mom got up at five-thirty A.M. right along with me in order to drive me to the rink. She never complained about it, in fact she was unfailingly cheerful as I dragged myself sleepily into the kitchen each morning. She would always be there with a smile and a cup of hot chocolate.

My schedule had to be tailored to fit the skating sessions. In order to be up early in the morning I had to be in bed by seven. Often I couldn't get to sleep. I would lie there listening to the sound of kids outside still playing. Downstairs the television was on and I could hear Mom cleaning up after dinner. When I finally managed to fall asleep Marcia would come clumping into the room and wake me up again. I used to think she did it on purpose, and maybe she did. In any case I grew so overtired that I began to fall asleep at my desk in class. The school was not sympathetic—they viewed it as a sign of inattention and no amount of explanation from my parents seemed to change their minds. So I just had to struggle to stay alert in class.

My increased ice time did begin to pay off, though. I took my Third Test and passed it with flying colors. Two double threes and two loops (difficult variations on the figure eight); two change threes and two change double threes, both consisting of three circles joined in a straight line. It was a much more difficult test than the second one. Passing it was exactly the encouragement I needed. I started to feel more cheerful and less hopeless. I began to believe in myself again.

As the winter wore on the grim prospect of patch grew increasingly difficult to face each morning. Mother and I made the long, dark drive to Rye speaking little and trying hard to stay awake. While I practiced my circles, tracing over and over the first figure, Mom would sit beside the ice patiently waiting for the two-hour session to end, sipping strong, hot coffee out of her thermos. Sometimes she read, often she just knit steadily, glancing up now and then to watch me squinting at the ice behind my blades, trying to see the etchings of my figures. Morning after morning I traced those endless circles, staring anxiously as the tracings unfolded, waiting for the one that would be finally perfect.

The shortage of ice was a problem and my mother and I drove

1967

around searching for places to practice my free skating. Then one day we spotted a strange tent-like structure built onto the side of the Showboat Restaurant in Greenwich, Connecticut. It turned out to be a small ice rink used for outdoor dining during the summer. The glass windows of the dining room looked into the tent so that the diners could watch the skaters. Most days there were very few brave souls willing to expose themselves to the critical eyes of the diners, but I didn't give it a thought. I put on my skates and took advantage of the ice. It was a very small surface—not big enough to do anything requiring speed. The roof was so low that a jump would have been impossible, so I did the best thing I could under those circumstances—I did a million spins. I did camels and laybacks, sit spins and scratch spins. That winter at the Showboat I learned to spin on the head of a dime.

In some ways the winter of 1967 was the hardest of my entire skating career. Fatigue made us all irritable and we squabbled constantly. Marcia was thirteen and had a host of friends and boundless enthusiasm for socializing. The family's attention was now centered around my skating and although she must have resented it in some ways, she liked the fact that it gave her the opportunity to come and go with a little more freedom than usual. She kept trying to entice me to join her at some of the parties she went to. But I was as shy as Marcia was outgoing and was only too glad to have an excuse to say no. After a while she stopped inviting me.

That spring I entered my second Wollman Open. I skated a program Barbara had choreographed for me and this time when the results were posted my name was on the top of the list. I had won my first gold medal and it made all the hard work seem worthwhile. Since Otto Gold was no longer teaching in Lake Placid, Barbara called the great Swiss coach, Gustave Lussi, to

Airborne at Wollman Rink

see if he would take me into his summer school. Mr. Lussi was one of the world's leading coaches at that time, having trained several Olympic winners and many World Champions. I was sure he wouldn't want to spend his time on a ten-year-old who still had no idea how to do a double axel. But I was wrong. Mr. Lussi accepted me, and in the early summer of 1967 I once again found myself heading for Lake Placid. I could hardly wait to get there and start to train again. I wanted to master a double axel and maybe even a triple jump, and I was sure Mr. Lussi would help me.

Gustave Lussi was a tall man who carried himself very erect and spoke with a noticeable Swiss accent. As I stood before him on my first morning at the ice rink he stared at me for a few moments, his brows knitted. At last he reached out his hand, spread the open palm beneath my chin and held it there.

"Spit it out!" he ordered.

33

I felt my chin quiver with fright. He continued to stare at me. "Well, young lady, I am waiting."

The eyes of all the other students were on me as I reddened with shame. Slowly I opened my mouth and spat out a large wad of pink gum. It landed in Mr. Lussi's open palm. He closed his hand over it, walked briskly to the garbage can and dropped it in. Then he took out an immaculate white handkerchief, wiped his hands thoroughly and walked back to me.

He looked at me again, not unkindly. "There are two things you will remember, Miss Hamill, if you are to study with me. First, you will never again chew gum. It is a disgusting habit with no possible redeeming quality. Second, you will remember at all times that you are a lady and you will conduct yourself accordingly." His steely blue eyes bored through me. "Is that understood?"

I nodded, not daring to speak. Suddenly he smiled broadly and motioned towards the ice. "Good. Then we will begin." From that moment on Gustave Lussi and I worked together in close harmony.

Gus Lussi always commanded total respect and obedience from his students. He had trained Dick Button when he won his two Olympic gold medals. Dick claimed that if Gus had ordered him to jump from a window he would have done so without hesitation—only he would have made sure his toe was pointed and his head was in the right position to achieve the maximum clearance. As I worked with Mr. Lussi I grew to understand exactly what Dick Button had meant. A great trainer will instill absolute trust in his students—a kind of blind faith and an unquestioning obedience.

I trusted Mr. Lussi implicitly and under his guidance my free skating began to take shape. I finally became consistent in my double salchow and double toe loop jumps. I learned complicated footwork and slowly started to work on a double axel. This was far more difficult than any other of the double jumps since it involved two-and-a-half revolutions in the air, but I was determined to master it.

Mr. Lussi took me aside one afternoon after my seventh fall. "You have to believe you can do it," he told me. "You have to have guts to be a great skater. You have to attack it with absolute confidence. If you hesitate you are lost. Go out there and give every move you do everything you've got."

I tried to follow his advice and although it wasn't always apparent that summer, it became the backbone of everything I have ever done in my life.

I passed my Fourth Test in early July. It was hard but I had been well prepared for it. It consisted of two double threes, two change threes, two brackets and two loops. All of these are variations on the basic figure eight but the changes of foot and edge are infinitely more complicated than those encountered in the earlier tests. I immediately began to train for my Fifth Test.

Mr. Lussi often used Gordie McKellen to demonstrate the correct way to execute jumps and I spent morning after morning happily gazing at Gordie's technical demonstrations. Mr. Lussi missed very little. One day he seemed particularly irritated and at the end of the free skating session he walked across to me, draped an arm lightly around my shoulders and guided me to the back of the rink. He turned to me with an almost imperceptible twinkle in his eyes.

"Dorothy," he said, "it will be as well for you to remember that when Mr. McKellen is showing you how to do a jump correctly, it is the legs and the arms you should watch, not the face." Then he walked quickly away.

Gordie McKellen was particularly helpful that summer. Besides training for the Senior competitions and giving demonstrations

35

to fledgling students, he took a serious interest in my skating. There was rarely a day when he didn't skate over to me and offer advice of one kind or another. We shared the same sense of humor and we began to build a friendship. Many times when I would be insecure about my skating or in a black mood Gordie would glide over and say something to make me laugh at myself. He had a marvelous sense of timing and an ability for mimicry that helped keep things in proper perspective. With Gordie around, it was impossible to take myself too seriously.

I TURNED eleven that July and my friends all gave me earrings—thirteen pairs in all. They were the first earrings I had ever owned and I was thrilled. There was only one problem. All the earrings were for pierced ears and my ears were still in one piece. I wrote my parents that I wanted to get my ears pierced. Cindy Kauffmann, who skated pairs with her brother Ron, had offered to pierce them for me but she said I had to get permission first.

In their next letter my folks ignored the request. I began to bombard them with letters begging for permission. My mom wrote back that she was delighted to receive so many letters from me (I had never been a good letter-writer) but that one thing concerned her. Nowhere in any of the letters had I mentioned anything about skating. I wrote back immediately that my skating was the best it had ever been and that I was enjoying it very much. But what about the ears? Back came the reply: No, you are too young. I was desperate. All my friends were walking around with pierced ears and all I could do with my treasured earrings was to sit them on my dresser and admire them.

Finally I hit on a scheme. The summer free skating competition was coming up. I had been a disaster at last year's competition and my parents were very anxious that I redeem myself this year. I wrote to them and proposed the first bargain I had ever made in my life: If I win the competition, may I get my ears pierced?

The reply was immediate: Yes. I was thrilled and started to work harder. A few days later a thought occurred to me. I wrote another letter: What if I come in second? The reply was swift: If you come second, then you can have one ear pierced. That seemed reasonable. But then I thought of something else. "Dear Mom," I wrote, "what happens if I come in third?" This time Dad replied. "If you come in third you can have your nose pierced." Fortunately it never came to that, because at that summer's end I won the free skating event and got both ears pierced.

Pierced ears!

FIVE

Moving On

$\mathcal{S}$KATING had taken over our lives. With the demands it placed on my parents' time, the household had to be arranged around my schedule. Marcia and I were always fighting—over our room, our clothes, conflicting interests and chores. We rarely spoke a civil word to one another. My brother Sandy was just turning fifteen, and his earlier passion for teasing me had lessened considerably. He was content with an occasional insult and could be counted on to throw just enough fuel on the fire to make sure it didn't actually go out. Otherwise he viewed the proceedings of our family from a detached point of view. He had just been accepted at Phillips Exeter Academy as a boarder and was getting ready to leave.

Sandy's real name is Chalmers, after my father. He was the brains of the family—not that the rest of us were lacking, but Sandy was the mad professor type, always experimenting with chemicals. He took such fiendish delight in frightening us all and had hinted so many times that he was making a bomb, that the day he came rushing up the basement stairs screaming for us to evacuate the house immediately, we did so without hesitation. We all stood outside on the lawn shivering, waiting for the house to blow up. When nothing happened we went back

Working with Barbara Taplan,
Riverdale, N.Y., 1968

inside but I slept fitfully that night, expecting to hear an explosion at any moment.

Sandy was also a genius at chess. When I was seven or eight he used to lock me into his room and make me play with him. Once, by sheer accident, I beat him—he was checkmated ten moves into the game. After that he refused to play with me again.

I was in tears the morning Sandy left for boarding school but I must admit the tears didn't last very long. As much as I loved him, his departure had one very positive aspect—Marcia and I, who for eleven years had been sharing a bedroom the size of a closet, suddenly had rooms of our own.

We spent Thanksgiving with Jonsie and Bill that year and as always, the warmth of their home enveloped us all, and seemed to pull us closer together. One evening we went to see *The Sound of Music* and I thought it the most wonderful movie I had ever seen. I had a very low opinion of my looks at that time and Julie Andrews represented everything that I admired and longed to be. Back at the house Jonsie said to me, "You know Dorothy, you look a little like Julie Andrews." I went upstairs and looked in the bedroom mirror for a long time. Jonsie had made me feel beautiful.

THAT CHRISTMAS I found among my presents an envelope containing tickets to the 1968 National Figure Skating Championships in Philadelphia. They were to be held the first week of February. My mom told me she felt it was time I went to see the Main Event. "Besides," she told me, "for once you can go to a competition and relax." I was thrilled. I would finally get to see John Misha Petkevich compete.

My parents and I drove down to Philadelphia on a gray morning and checked into the official hotel for the Championships.

Right away I caught the excitement in the air. I made my mother sit in the lobby for over an hour while I watched eagerly as the skaters arrived and registered. Each time I spotted a famous face I would dart from my hiding place and thrust my autograph book out to be signed. Finally my mother took me by the hand and insisted we go to lunch.

The finals of the Ladies' Championship were held on the Saturday evening. I watched in awe as I saw Janet Lynn skate for the first time. I will never forget the moment she came out onto the ice. A hush fell over the arena. People held their breath. She radiated a kind of magic—she glowed as she skated, seeming to float effortlessly above the ice. I was entranced.

Janet, however, did not win. The gold medal went to Peggy Fleming who was already a two-time World Champion and, at eighteen, the favorite to win the Winter Olympics later that month. Peggy looked radiant and from the moment she began to skate there was never any doubt that she would win. I only realized in later years how fortunate I was to have seen her there, because it was to be her last competition in this country.

As she turned to face us at the end of her number, I tugged at my mom's sleeve. "Someday can I have a dress just like Peggy's?" I asked.

Mom smiled at me. "Someday. And someday you'll be able to skate just like Peggy, too."

I told her I didn't want to skate like Peggy Fleming.

She looked surprised. "You like Janet better?" she asked.

I shook my head. "They're both wonderful, but I don't want to skate like them. I want to skate like John Misha Petkevich."

I MADE slow, steady progress all through the spring of 1968. As my skating improved, my school work deteriorated. I had to miss the first twenty minutes of class each day because of patch and I had a seat in the back of the class so that I could slip in without causing a disturbance. I wasn't doing well at all. I had difficulty seeing the blackboard from back there, but I was afraid to tell the teacher. She didn't like me very much and didn't approve of my being allowed to come to school late. As the months went on I became more and more frustrated. I would sit at my desk with eyes heavy with sleep and fight to concentrate. But it was hopeless. I always ended up drifting off into a daydream.

One day during class, the slow drone of the teacher's voice soothed me. I felt my head nodding forward onto my book.

"Dorothy Hamill!"

I came to and looked up to see her advancing toward me menacingly. I knew I must have done something to upset her but had no idea what it was. As she reached my desk she grabbed me and pulled me from my seat. "When I call on you, you will answer me. Is that understood?"

I nodded, too miserable to speak. This only served to infuriate her more. She shook me violently and I heard my dress rip. All the way home that afternoon I worried about what to tell my mother about the dress. I was afraid to say the teacher did it because she might complain to the school; then the teacher would take it out on me. In the end I told her I caught it on a nail.

THAT SUMMER I returned to Lake Placid for my third year in a row. It was becoming a second home to me. Gus Lussi taught me a double lutz and a double flip, and although they weren't always consistent, I did land them more often than not. The lutz was the first reverse jump I had ever done, jumping counter-clockwise from a left back outside edge. The toepick of the free foot is used to assist in takeoff and

I kept sliding off the pick. The flip jump is approached from a shallow left forward inside edge. The takeoff position is complicated but for some reason I didn't seem to find it particularly difficult.

Mr. Lussi had his own method of encouraging new achievements in the world of jumps. He set out a row of quarters and dimes along the barriers. "Each time you land a new jump without error, one of these coins will be yours," he said, waving his hand towards the barrier. "For a lutz you get a quarter. For a flip, ten cents. For a double axel, you get two quarters."

I was intent on winning those coins. I tried for days and finally, on the same afternoon, I landed a perfect double lutz and a perfect double flip. I got the quarter and the dime, but I

Lake Placid trophy, 1968

Practicing at Riverdale, 1968

didn't spend them. I took them home instead and taped them to a card. To this day they remain in a frame on my bedroom wall.

At the end of the summer I passed my Fifth Test. Besides including a variety of change loops, change double threes and brackets, the Fifth Test also includes a one-foot eight. This is a figure requiring immense control of the skating knee as the entire figure is skated on one foot only.

The end-of-summer free skating competition in Lake Placid, although not a qualifying event, is considered an important measure of a skater's standing before going into the new competitive season. Mr. Lussi allowed me to enter the Intermediate free skating competition. I placed third and felt I had done reasonably well for my first competition at that level. I was devastated, therefore, when Mr. Lussi called me over on the last morning of the summer session and told me I shouldn't be competing at the Intermediate level. My heart sank into my boots. I stared at him in disbelief and felt tears at the back of my eyes. I *couldn't* have been that bad. . . .

Suddenly he smiled. "You're still very small," he said slowly, "but I think—if you're prepared to work very hard—you could be ready for Novice level. I will speak to your parents about it."

He turned on his heel and strode quickly away. I stared after him, dazed. I had jumped a whole level in one summer. With luck I could be in the running for the next Nationals.

Gustave Lussi

School photo

BACK IN CONNECTICUT Barbara doubled her efforts with me. The prospect of competing in the Novice Championship was scary but I figured I would just go in and do my very best. The North Atlantics were to be in Rochester, New York, at the end of November. Technically I was at about the same level as most of the other girls competing in the Novice event. But my lack of performing experience hurt me in the free skating. I skated well but I was clearly not the best. The girl who won—Debbie Milne—skated an outstanding program. I watched her admiringly and when she came off the ice I told her how much I had enjoyed her performance. She smiled and offered to buy me a Coke. That day the two of us became both friends and arch rivals. I finished third, qualifying for the Eastern Sectionals, and went home to Connecticut with my bronze medal in my suitcase and Debbie's phone number in my pocket.

Barbara Taplan moved from the rink in Rye to another rink in Riverdale, New York—a neighborhood on the northern edge of New York City. The new ice rink had open sides and as fall gave way to winter, skating there was a little like being inside a refrigerator. The wind whistled through the building, swirling around us as we skated. It was freezing.

In the early dawn I could look out at big apartment buildings and see the warm yellow squares of people's kitchen windows begin to light up. I traced my eternal figures imagining coffee pots bubbling on stoves. But it was the smells that really got to me. There was a bakery nearby and when the wind was right, the aroma of fresh-baked bagels drifted into the rink. Every morning Mom marched up and down the edge of the rink in order to keep her blood moving. Finally she would disappear and come back with a large brown paper sack. It was bagel time. Later she'd go to the car, turn on the engine, the radio

Now a Novice, Riverdale, 1968

and the heater and read the morning paper, while she thawed.

One particularly vicious morning when I was rigid with cold and my teeth had started to chatter uncontrollably, I skated over to the side of the ice to warm my hands around a cup of hot chocolate. Another student was standing there, rubbing her hands together and groaning softly. "I think they're dead," she said. Then she looked at me and shook her head. "Why do we do it—why do we torture ourselves like this?"

"Because we are mad," I answered, "stark, raving mad."

I WENT to study with Gus Lussi over the Christmas vacation. Lake Placid looked very different from the way I remembered it. The village looked like a Christmas card with the bare branches of trees outlined sharply against the blue winter sky. The lake was a sheet of milk-white ice, broken here and there by skate tracks or footprints. The houses huddled together under blankets of snow and people walked about the streets stamping their feet and clapping their mittened hands together, their breath emerging in tiny, white streams of thin cloud.

This visit I stayed at McKellen's Pine Lodge, the hotel run by Gordie's father. To my disappointment I saw nothing of Gordie because he was spending the Christmas vacation training at the Wagon Wheel in Rockford, Illinois. But I was excited about this opportunity to work with Mr. Lussi again and was determined to work very hard on my jumps. The patch sessions were as boring as always until one particular afternoon when I came off the ice to buy a Tab at the refreshment stand. Instead of the pleasant older man who usually ran it, a boy not much older than me stood behind the counter.

"Hi!" he said, grinning and holding out his hand in a grand gesture. "I'm David. I'm running the stand for my dad while he's away." I was impressed. He had the bluest eyes I had ever seen and I thought him very handsome. All of a sudden the Olympic Arena took on a rosy glow.

Towards the end of the week, two days before New Year's,

David called me at the Lodge. In a carefully off-hand voice he
asked if I would care to spend New Year's Eve with him, or if I
already had plans. I made no attempt to invent any—although
Marcia always told me I should never be too eager with boys.
This was the first time anyone had ever asked me out and I
wasn't going to take any chances on scaring him off. I assured
him I had no plans at all and that I would love to spend New
Year's Eve with him. He sounded relieved and his voice became
hearty. He would pick me up at the Lodge around eight o'clock
if that would suit me.

"You drive?" I asked, impressed. I'd had no idea he was that
old.

He cleared his throat uncomfortably. "Well—no, not exactly.
You see, my dad will be driving us."

I spent a long time worrying about what to wear. I tried on
one thing after another but nothing looked right. David was
taking me to the Lake Placid Country Club and I had no idea
what would be appropriate. I was sure I would look out of place
and ruin the evening. In the end I decided on the only long
dress I owned—it was black with a white collar trimmed with
lace and appliquéd with cherries.

When the car arrived to pick me up my knees were shaking
and I hoped no one would notice. David was very formal as he
introduced me to his father, who was actually an old buddy of
mine from the concession stand.

David's father left us at the door after we promised not to be
out too late. David and I held hands all night, feeling very
grownup and slightly breathless. We danced a lot, not very
expertly but with increasing abandon. When midnight arrived
David ventured a cautious kiss to welcome in the New Year.
When finally we walked home, plowing our way through the
snowy streets, I hardly noticed the cold. I was glowing.

Training with Sonya, 1969

Nothing to Lose

I PLACED fifth in school figures at Easterns. Debbie Milne was in the lead. We were both well positioned to repeat our regional standings. Before the long program, which counted for fifty percent of the overall mark, my parents had a meeting with Sonya Klopfer Dunfield, a former National Champion and Olympic competitor and a prominent teacher at the Skating Club of New York. I had already been working with Sonya on my school figures, and she told my parents she was impressed with my showing in Rochester. She said I had an excellent chance of moving into the medals at Easterns and then would be able to compete in the Nationals.

Debbie and I both skated well in the free skating. Once again she finished first and I was third. As we stood on the podium to receive our medals Debbie winked and said, "See you in Seattle."

When I got home I sensed something was afoot. Finally Mom told me that she and Dad had decided I needed to move on to another coach—that perhaps Barbara had taken me as far as I could go with her. They wanted me to start training with Sonya Dunfield. I was sick about it, not because I didn't respect Sonya, but because I loved Barbara dearly. I didn't want to hurt her. She had brought me right to the brink of the National Championships and it just didn't seem right to desert her at this point.

I didn't know how Barbara would take the news. But when my mother told her, she said she thought it an excellent idea and that if I ever needed her she would always be there for me.

She invited me to her house that night as a sort of farewell gesture. We ate dinner and watched TV and talked, as we had so many times before. On this occasion we deliberately avoided discussing skating. When it was finally time to go to bed, Barbara turned to me and spoke slowly, choosing her words carefully as she told me not to feel sad. It was time for me to move on. She wanted me to move forward eagerly, to learn all I could from anyone who could teach me. She assured me that Sonya was an excellent teacher and that I would be in good hands with her.

She paused a moment before finishing. "Just remember—however far up the ladder you go, I will always be proud of the part I played in helping you."

There were tears in her eyes—not to mention mine—and she hugged me. "It's time to take the next step, Dorothy."

THE National Championships were only three weeks off, and I began to train with Sonya right away. She worked with me at my home club in Rye, New York, for three hours a day, concentrating mostly on my school figures. As they improved, so did my confidence. I began to look forward to Seattle.

One Saturday morning I came downstairs to find my mother with her coat already on.

"Hurry Dorothy," she said. "We don't have much time if we're going into New York."

I was puzzled. "Why are we going to New York?" I asked.

Mom smiled. "Because it's time you had a real skating dress—one like Peggy Fleming's."

Mom had found a French dressmaker in Manhattan who did the most exquisite beadwork. She designed a dress for me that morning and promised it would be ready in time for the Nationals.

"What color do you like best?" she asked me.

"Green," I said without hesitation.

A week later we were on our way back for the final fitting. When the dress was taken out of its wrappings I gasped. I'd never seen anything so beautiful. Under the lights the pale-green sequined moons shimmered like magic. I could hardly wait to wear it.

Just before Nationals my parents had another conference with Sonya. She assured them that I was as well prepared as possible. "The rest," she told them, "is up to Dorothy."

Sonya took me to Seattle. I was glad she would be there—it made me feel secure. Later Dad told me that he and Mom had decided to bring Marcia.

"You're all coming?" I asked in surprise.

Dad grinned. "You think we'd miss this one?"

When we got to Seattle I saw Debbie Milne down at the practice rink and she invited me to have a soda with her.

I shook my head. "No time," I said. "But thanks anyway. Maybe we can do it later."

I was remembering Mr. Lussi's advice to me just before I left Lake Placid at Christmas time. "There are two rules you must always follow when you compete," he said. "One—never make friends with your competitors until after the event is over. Until then you need all your concentration for skating. Two—no matter how you feel, you are never too ill to skate. Somehow you will be able to get through it."

It wasn't long before Mr. Lussi's second rule was put to the test. On the morning of school figures I woke up feeling peculiar. Not exactly ill, but decidedly off-color. I didn't feel like skating. My father felt my forehead. It wasn't hot. Mom decided that whatever was wrong with me was psychological. Sonya told me to get up. "You will be just fine once you get going," she assured me. So I skated, but my performance in school figures was dismal. I finished in sixth place. My parents were terribly disappointed. They had hoped that after all the extra training, I would move up a place or two. Sonya tried to encourage them. She felt that I was strong enough as a free skater to pull up into the medals, as I had done in Easterns.

About an hour before I had to leave for the free skating competition, I put on my coat and went out for a long walk. It was a brilliantly sunny day and snow gleamed on the peaks of the Olympic Mountains. I thought Seattle must be the most beautiful city I had ever seen. The air was crisp and clean and I breathed it deeply. As I walked I made promises to myself—I would make my parents proud of me; I would land all my jumps correctly so I could call Mr. Lussi and he would be pleased; I would remember all of Sonya's instructions. At last, convinced that all was in order, I went back to the hotel and changed. The new green dress fit perfectly.

Just before I was announced to skate, something happened to me that I had never experienced before. I got stage fright. The prospect of ten thousand people waiting to see me skate suddenly seemed overwhelming. I turned to Sonya in a panic. "I can't do this—I can't go out there," I said.

I could hear my name being carried over the loud speakers and people beginning to applaud. My heart stopped. I felt my skin prickle. Sonya put a firm but gentle hand on my shoulder and turned me around to face the arena again. "You can't quit

Spiral, Toronto, 1969

now Dorothy," she said. "Just forget everything except the ice."

And with that she gave me a push. I found myself traveling toward the center ice and taking up my position facing the judges. I thought of the advice another skater had given me earlier that day—a very good free skater—after she had done poorly in figures. "I don't have anything to lose now Dorothy," she had said, "so I'm just going to go out there and enjoy myself." And that's exactly what she had done, right before me. She had given a marvelous performance and pulled right into third place.

As a hush fell over the arena my music began. I felt the fear drain from me. I took a deep breath and energy began to flood through me. I was going to be all right.

I skated well, as well as I knew how, and landed my double lutz jump with ease. I was beginning to enjoy myself. I did the layback spin and heard the applause rippling as I came out of it. I was almost at the end of my program and was so elated with the way things were going, that I lost my concentration for a moment—a moment is all it takes. As I landed my double toe loop jump I lost control of my edge and sat down on the ice. I recovered almost in one movement and went on to finish with a flourish right in front of the judges' stand. I came off the ice and saw Sonya smiling at me.

"How was it?" I asked.

She hugged me. "You did well," she said. "I'm proud of you."

The marks came up and they were very strong. I was the last skater out and I waited for an announcement of the final standings. I thought that I might have pulled into fourth. My dad, who is always faster than the official scorekeepers, came rushing towards me and lifted me up in the air.

"You did it!" he shouted.

"Did what?"

"You won—you're the Novice Champion!"

I was stunned. Happiness flooded through me in a great wave. I had won a National Championship and all I could think about was that now I would get one of those pins.

A tiny gold skate blade with a single diamond set into the toe is given by the United States Figure Skating Association to the winners of a National Championship. I had wanted one of those pins ever since I saw Peggy Fleming wearing hers in Philadelphia. At the Gala Reception on Saturday evening I was announced as the Novice Champion. I floated up to the head table with my

Novice Champion, Seattle, 1969, with Juli McKinstry, left, and Sheri Thrapp

cheeks burning and my heart pumping, and when the president of the Association pinned the little gold blade onto my dress, I couldn't have been happier if I had just been crowned a princess. I threaded my way back to my table and on the way I caught sight of Gordie.

"You've beaten the women," he teased. "Now when are you gonna take on the men?"

Toronto, 1969

SEVEN

Back to Basics

ACK home in Connecticut my skating club held a reception in my honor. The president made a speech and presented me with a money tree. It was something the club did for its top competitive skaters in order to help defray the expenses. Every club member had contributed a five or ten dollar bill which had been folded to make the leaves of the tree. There must have been more than two hundred dollars on that tree. I was excited and spent the rest of the evening planning how I would spend it all. My mom, however, had other ideas. When we got into the car to drive home she held out her hand for the tree. "But I was going to buy clothes with it," I said sadly.

Mom looked at me for a moment and then pulled out two ten dollar bills. "Here," she said. "These are for you. The rest will buy six more skating lessons."

The cost of my skating career had begun to escalate. I was aware that it was expensive, but my parents never once in all the years I was an amateur let me know just how severe a drain it was on their resources. If I had known, I might have insisted on giving up long before the Olympics.

My parents financed education and training for all three of us kids as long as we worked at our chosen fields and pulled our weight along the way. We all had to do our share of the chores but we were never made to feel guilty about what things cost. We were asked to appreciate the opportunities we were given— and to make the most of them.

Looking back, however, I can see the costs must have been enormous. By this time I was skating every day except Saturday. A normal public practice session cost anywhere from three to six dollars an hour, and I needed about twenty hours a week. Private lessons cost between fifteen and thirty dollars an hour depending on the coach. Gas to drive to and from the rinks and the cost of blade sharpening made up the balance of the day-to-day expenses. Before my amateur years were over, expenses would increase to staggering proportions.

AFTER THE Nationals I continued to skate patch each morning at the Riverdale Rink, getting up at five A.M. in order to be on the ice at six. Because of this I still observed a very early curfew and was in bed most evenings by seven. I resented it. I was twelve years old, and everyone else my age was going to movies and parties and hanging out together in the evenings. I was ashamed of being in bed so early and scared that someone would find out and make fun of me. When my friends called after seven, I made my mom tell them that I was out. Only my best friend Kim knew the truth, and as far as I knew she never told anyone. I got the reputation of leading a very wild and secret social life.

On Sundays I continued to work with Sonya Dunfield and her husband Peter, a former Canadian World competitor. Their home rink, housed in the old Madison Square Garden, had just been torn down, and the new facility—Skyrink—would not be ready till the fall of 1969. In the interim they rented ice at various rinks in the New York-New Jersey area. Sonya suggested that my mom and dad bring me to her house on Saturday afternoons and let me spend the night. So every Saturday at four o'clock my parents and I set off for the Dunfields' in Creskill, New Jersey. This weekly ritual became a source of pleasure to my parents, as they made a point of stopping on their way back for a long, leisurely dinner at an old country inn they'd discovered on their first trip.

I enjoyed those weekends also, at least the Saturday evenings. Sonya's mother, who lived with them, was a great cook. We ate marvelous dinners, watched a little television and then all went to bed while the birds were still singing. Because the rink was a two-hour drive from their house, we had to leave at four A.M. in order to get there for six o'clock patch. Sonya and I used to sleep soundly while poor Peter did the driving.

We skated patch from six to eight A.M. at the Bricktown Rink, took a ten-minute break while the ice was resurfaced, then free skated for another hour. These punishing early morning sessions were far worse than anything I had done before and I was so numb from fatigue and cold that I skated in a kind of semi-coma.

As soon as the free skate was over at nine A.M., we would leap into Peter's car again and drive at top speed to the West New York Rink where we managed to get another two hours of free skating in from ten to twelve. The rink was in a horrible neighborhood so we were always a little uneasy there. But ice was ice—you took it anywhere you could get it. At noon Dad would pull up in his car to take me home and I would drag myself wearily into the front seat, turn on the radio and fall asleep.

In February Sonya invited me to go to the New York City

Ballet with her. I had only seen ballet on television so I was very excited. We met at the fountains in the courtyard of Lincoln Center. The whole evening was enchanted. I held my breath as the heavy curtains swept up towards the ceiling and revealed the vast expanse of stage. The ballet was "Dances at a Gathering." It was not a story ballet like "Swan Lake" or "Giselle" but was very modern and sometimes even bizarre. I loved every second of it.

It occurred to me more than once during the evening that this ballet could have been even more effective if done on ice. I was sensing instinctively the great sweep of ice and the long, flowing lines that are possible on blades. The great impresario, Sol Hurok, once said that to put an ice skater on the stage would be like putting a racehorse into a kitchen—ridiculous. Mr. Hurok certainly knew more about theater than Dorothy Hamill, but I disagreed with him and silently vowed that I would one day prove him wrong.

In spite of the inconvenience of training with Sonya and Peter I felt I was beginning to make substantial headway. I had developed my ability to execute connecting footwork between my free skating moves—an area in which I had always been weak—and I began to learn more about overall performing as opposed to straight technique, and my figures improved steadily. I passed my Sixth Test. Suddenly everything was beginning to come together.

SONYA AND PETER wanted me to go to Toronto for a summer session at the famous Cricket Skating and Curling Club. They always took their top students there for summer training. My mother had hoped I would stay closer to home so that I could do some other things besides skate—we kept a boat at the yacht club and I was still a moderately good swimmer—but the potential benefits of the Cricket Club were irresistible. Finally she gave in, and at the end of July I was on a plane with Sonya bound for Toronto.

The Cricket Club was set back from Avenue Road in the north Toronto area. It had one of the finest private rinks anywhere. Above the ice was a formal dining room and cocktail lounge with a floor-to-ceiling glass wall overlooking the rink. Here parents could sit in comfort watching their aspiring champions and enjoying a quiet drink.

Just before leaving for Toronto I had bought new skates, and I was having terrible trouble trying to break them in. I have an extra bone on my ankle that tends to rub against the stiff new leather and hurt me, so Mom had always taken new boots into a repair shop and used a bunion punch to push the leather out at the point of the bone. This time, however, that hadn't helped.

By the end of my second week in Toronto I could hardly walk. My feet were covered with blisters and sore places. I stuffed my boots with foam rubber but it did no good. Finally I broke down in tears and told Sonya I couldn't stand it any longer. She examined my feet and my boots carefully. "You need Stanzione's boots," she said. "He'll fit your boots properly and you'll be surprised how much better your feet will feel."

The following morning Sonya and I flew down to New York to G. Stanzione, the custom boot shop. My feet were so sore by this time that I would have given anything to find a pair of boots that didn't hurt me.

I arrived at Mr. Stanzione's shop looking so forlorn that he sat me down instantly and looked critically at my feet. He examined them from every angle, noting the unusual lumps and the extra ankle bone. He saw the huge blisters and the places

where the new boots cut into my flesh. "No wonder your feet hurt," he said kindly. "All this . . ." He waved a hand at my feet. He explained that in order to fit properly, boots had to be made from molds of an individual's feet so that they were exactly the right shape in every part. He began to measure me, making patterns of my feet. He told me stories about famous skaters and the problems they had with their feet. He knew about everybody's feet.

He told me about one skater who had figured out a way to break in his new boots quickly. He put them on, then immersed his feet in hot water until the boots were thoroughly soaked

Breaking in new skates,
Toronto, 1969

through. Then he went to bed still wearing them and let them dry right on his feet. This worked wonders for the boots—they fit perfectly. But the skater died of pneumonia.

A week later my new boots were in Toronto. To my dismay, they felt like two blocks of concrete. Sonya tried to soothe me, explaining that it would still take a while to break them in. The difference was that these boots wouldn't cut me. They would break in evenly. She was right. After two weeks they began to feel pretty good and after four they were the best boots I had ever had. Since then I always bought my boots at Mr. Stanzione's.

At the very end of August I took my Seventh Canadian Test and passed it with flying colors. Sonya took me out for dinner to celebrate. Then I went down to Buffalo to take my Seventh Test under U.S.F.S.A. rules. This test required one-foot eights, which are very difficult, being skated all on one foot; two change loops and two paragraph threes; and four rockers which consist of three circles joined at the top and bottom. Again I passed and I was thrilled.

IN SEPTEMBER I went back to Lake Placid to skate in the Labor Day show and to work on my double axle with Gus Lussi. The Labor Day show went well, but the double axel was not so easy to conquer.

As usual, Mr. Lussi laid out two quarters side by side on the barrier before we started each session. I was determined to win them. But I just couldn't seem to get the jump right. It was a very difficult jump which involved two-and-a-half revolutions in the air. The more frustrated I became, the more I fell. I was black and blue from falling—so bruised I couldn't walk properly. One day my parents came to pick me up after one of these sessions and I couldn't get into the car. I simply couldn't lift my left leg—my knee refused to bend properly. Every time I tried I could feel pains like red hot needles. I was in agony.

My mother was impatient. "It can't be all that bad, Dorothy," she said. But it was that bad. And to make matters worse, I seemed to be farther away from landing the jump than ever. Later my mom saw the bruises and understood why I was so upset. She put an arm around me and said she was sorry. "I can't take the bruises away," she said. "Only time will do that. But you must decide if you really think this is all worth it. Even after you have mastered the double axel there will be triple jumps. It won't get any easier, you know."

I nodded. I knew she was right and I also knew that I was fully prepared to accept the inevitable aches and bruises. Just so long as I could continue to skate.

I wonder, looking back on that summer, whether it would be any easier if I were training today. The kids wear pads to learn jumps, and they don't get nearly as sore. But somehow I think I might have been lucky not to have had them—it would have been too easy to become dependent on them.

Eventually I did manage a double axel and I got the two quarters. Mr. Lussi immediately replaced them with three quarters. "For the first perfect triple salchow," he told me. And so it began again—the wind-up, the jump, the fall. A continuous cycle. But I was making progress. Only a year before, Mr. Lussi had told me I could compete as a Novice. Now at thirteen, I was National Novice Champion and had passed all but one of the figure tests. It had been an eventful year.

EIGHT

A Taste of Politics

*T*HE Skyrink opened in the fall of 1969 on the sixteenth floor of an office building near the center of Manhattan. Sonya and Peter Dunfield were both given teaching tenure there and I began to work with them on a daily basis. It was a long drive from home to New York City—an hour and a half each way—and we still had to start before dawn in order to get an early patch session. I remember playing the car radio to keep me awake, turning up the volume and singing the words of all the hit tunes until Mom begged for mercy. Compared to the Riverdale Rink, Skyrink was heaven. It was warm and comfortable, and within weeks was attracting prominent skaters from all over the country.

One of the first visitors, to my delight, was Gordie McKellen. He came into Skyrink one morning with two large suitcases and announced he was coming to stay at my house. "Your folks have invited me," he said. We started spending a great deal of time together. We went for long walks and held hands. We went to drive-in's and held hands (Gordie had a car by this time). But since we never actually discussed the fact that we were holding hands I wasn't even sure if he liked me. I only knew that I liked him. One night he took me to see the movie *Love Story* and

1970

when it was over and the lights went up, we found we had both been crying. We laughed at one another and Gordie suggested a hamburger. Seated in McDonald's, he reached across the table and took my hand.

"You know, Dot," he said, "I really like you." I smiled at him.

"Me, too," I said happily. He took a bite of his Big Mac and chewed for a moment.

"No—I mean I really *like* you," he persisted. I held my breath, unsure of what I was supposed to say next. I said nothing. I was afraid to spoil the moment.

Gordie drained his Coke and stood up. "Come on," he said, taking my hand. "Let's go for a drive." I followed willingly.

We drove around for a while (it was raining, of course) and finally he parked the car and turned on the radio. He took my hand and we kissed a little and then he leaned back in his seat.

"Dot," he said solemnly, "I want to talk to you." He looked at me searchingly. "I don't want you to take this the wrong way . . . I mean, I don't know how to put this."

"I won't take it wrong," I assured him. "I promise. What is it?"

He cleared his throat. "Well," he said slowly, "it's about your double flip—it needs some work."

I let out my breath. So much for my romance.

I WAS HAVING problems with the other girls at the New York Skating Club. They resented me, feeling I had been admitted only because I was the Novice Champion. To them I was an outsider—a rival—and I could feel the air crackle every time I walked into the dressing room. Sometimes I would catch them making faces behind my back.

There was one girl in particular who upset me more than the

rest. She was pretty, vivacious and had an everlasting supply of beautiful clothes. She was also a very good skater and would be one of the leading contenders for the North Atlantics later in the fall. She never missed an opportunity to make a joke at my expense, and in club competitions she and I would fight hard to outdo one another. We quickly became enemies.

One day I was shopping with my mom when I noticed a Head ski jacket in a store window. It was white with a beautiful fox fur collar. I showed it to my mom who assured me that she would love to buy it for me but couldn't afford it right now. I understood but I couldn't stop thinking about it. I stood and gazed longingly at it every time I passed the store.

"Could I have it for Christmas?" I asked one day.

Mom shook her head. "I wish I could say yes, Dorothy, but I can't. Not this year. It's ninety dollars."

I talked about the coat at the club and described what it looked like. My arch rival overheard the conversation and a week later she came in Skyrink wearing the coveted jacket. I was crushed. When I went home and told my mother, she was full of sympathy, knowing the kind of social pressures that existed in the club, but was unable to do anything to help.

A PROMINENT MEMBER of the Skating Club of New York, Mrs. Ellen Long, was concerned about the three hours of driving my mom and I put in each day and offered to let me stay in her apartment in Manhattan whenever I wanted to. She was in Florida for the winter, but there was a staff in the apartment to look after me. The suggestion was a welcome one, and we quickly took advantage of it. I still went to school in Connecticut, but we agreed that sometimes I would stay over on a Friday and spend Saturday at the rink.

The first time I went back to the apartment from the rink I

could hardly believe what I saw. It was a whole city block long, on the fashionable Upper East Side near Central Park. I had had no idea that anyone lived in such an enormous place. To me it looked exactly like a museum, but I loved being there. There was a housekeeper who made sure I got up in time to go skating in the morning and a cook who made the meals. I slept in a beautiful bedroom like something out of one of my romantic dreams. It was like living in a different world.

THE NORTH ATLANTICS were in Buffalo in November, and I was competing for the first time as a Junior. Sonya was there with two other girls from the New York Skating Club. I didn't see very much of her that competition, and Dad supervised my practice sessions. When I skated figures I surprised everyone, including myself, by finishing in third place. My spirits soared. I had a chance at a medal and worked feverishly at practice that afternoon. The following morning Dad drove me across the Canadian border to Fort Erie where he had located some ice I could use for a couple of hours practice.

The rink was open-sided so the wind cut across the ice. It was freezing cold but I couldn't jump with my coat on, so I took it off and pulled on a thick button-up sweater. I started to skate as I was fastening it. I was wearing a big fur hat and had my head down as I fumbled with the last button. I was going very fast by now. I thought I could hear someone shouting, but the wind made it impossible to be sure. The last button closed, I looked up just in time to see a rope stretched right across the rink at chest height. I was approaching it much too fast to be able to stop, so I put up my hands instinctively to grab it. The speed at which I hit caused me to catapult backwards onto the ice with great force. I hit my head very hard and blacked out.

The next thing I knew people were dragging me off the ice and laying me out on a bench. I heard my dad's voice calling anxiously to me; someone was rubbing my hands. I opened my eyes. My head throbbed and my vision was blurred. I could see two of everyone.

Tears started to pour down my face and I heard Dad ask, "Dorothy—what is it?"

"My head," I sobbed. "It hurts so bad." But it wasn't just the pain in my head. It was everything. I had been doing so well—I had been in sight of the gold medal. And now some sixth sense told me I wasn't going to be able to skate tomorrow. I was going to be eliminated from the competition.

Back in Buffalo a doctor came to my room and examined me carefully. He was one of the U.S.F.S.A. officials, and he knew how much this competition meant to me. But when he had finished checking me over he shook his head. "I'm afraid you can't let Dorothy skate tomorrow," he told my parents. "Even if she feels all right, she could have some residual effect and black out in the middle of a jump. It would be very dangerous. She could kill herself."

I heard what he said, but I was determined to finish the competition.

My head stopped aching and only a large egg remained to show that anything had happened at all, but my parents were adamant. They wouldn't hear of me skating again until I had had x-rays in New York and they could be sure I was all right. They scratched my name from the event and the next morning I was in the car on my way home. I couldn't even stay and watch the rest of the competitions.

I stared out the window all the way back but saw nothing. Everything was a blur to me, and all I could think of was how well I had been doing and how cruel life could be. "I felt sure I would win," I said miserably. "Now I can't even get into Easterns."

My mom told me that Sonya thought I would get a bye into Easterns. I was not to be comforted. I didn't want a bye—I wanted to win my way in, fair and square. X-rays confirmed the next day that there was no serious damage, and a week later I received official confirmation that I had indeed been granted a bye into Easterns.

IN DECEMBER I was training harder than ever, and Sonya gave me a great deal of attention. She wanted to make sure I was all right after the accident. The other girls were hostile. They still treated me as an outsider and were not about to welcome me into their circle just because I had bumped my head. I felt the dirty looks exchanged behind my back. I was miserable.

One day, just before Easterns, Sonya called out to me as I was leaving. "Come with me and I'll buy you a hot chocolate. I want to talk to you."

We walked together through the snow and found a diner two blocks away from the rink. Sonya told me that she knew what I was going through with the other girls, but that I would have to accept it, to learn to live with it.

"As long as you are successful there will be people who resent you for it," she said. "Nothing you can do or say will ever change that." She looked at me seriously. "I want you to understand that, because I believe you are going all the way to the top and you're going to have to deal with this sort of thing a lot. Just don't ever take it personally. Be proud of what you've achieved. Believe in yourself and what you do."

I felt better listening to Sonya. I felt my strength and determination returning. Sonya was right.

EASTERNS WERE in Boston, and we arrived with a heavy snow falling. The first person I saw as we checked into the hotel was my arch rival from the Skyrink, resplendent in her new Head ski jacket. She had come in second in North Atlantics, thereby qualifying for Easterns. Later I ran into Debbie Milne, who had won and was a strong favorite to take the Easterns. She put her hand on my arm and said, "I want you to know I wish you luck, Dorothy. That was a rotten thing that happened to you in Buffalo."

The figures did not go well for me. I finished in fifth position. But the free skating was another matter. I skated better than ever before in my life and passed Debbie to take first place. I was the Junior gold medalist.

Training for the Tulsa Nationals

Nationals that year were held in Tulsa, Oklahoma, and I was ready for them. I was third after school figures and Sonya was ecstatic. I was, she felt, perfectly placed to move up. The free skating competition went smoothly. I skated as well as I knew how, and as I came off the ice Sonya gave me a hug. "I think you did it!" she said.

But it was not to be. I got my first taste of skating politics that day. In spite of a good performance I was awarded mediocre marks and finished second to Juli McKinstry.

The judging process in amateur competitions has always been a subject of controversy. Particularly at the all-important international events, judges appear to play favorites, sometimes awarding unreasonably high marks to skaters from their own countries. Skating is a subjective sport—there is no stopwatch or finish line to determine the absolute winner. Judges are bound to be influenced by many different factors. I think even sentiment may play a part at times. Certainly taste differs from judge to judge. One may lean towards the strong, athletic performances; another may favor the balletic grace of the more artistic skaters. But I have no doubt that the overwhelming factor is always political.

As a competitor there is nothing a skater can do about the judging. Judges are autonomous and there is no effective appeal system. Throughout history there have been great skaters who have tried to buck the system—to protest—but, so far as I can remember, none of them has ever won a world title. In the end, the best way to get on is to accept defeat gracefully. I felt I had skated well that day in Tulsa, and although I was bitterly disappointed with the marks the judges had given me, I looked ahead to the next competition. I had to keep believing in myself and remembering that there would always be another chance.

As I came out of the dressing room after the free skating, my mom came up with something draped over her arm. It was the Head ski jacket with the fox collar—the one I had coveted since the fall. She put it around my shoulders and gave me a hug. "I didn't quite make it for Christmas," she said, "but I think it was worth waiting for."

I WAS in seventh grade that spring, and even though I had missed weeks of school, Mom was trying hard to keep me up to date. She especially wanted me to take part in the normal school activities. There was a seventh grade spring dance coming up and I was determined to go. I had a big crush on one of the guys in my class and I planned to wear a new dress Jonsie had given me—pink and very pretty, I thought.

Mom told me I could go, but that I had to be home by eight o'clock to go to bed. That was an hour extension on my normal bedtime that spring. Usually I didn't mind the early curfew, but once in a while it got to me and I felt deprived. But Mom knew that if she didn't insist—that if she broke the rules even once—everything would become much more difficult.

The night of the dance Dad drove me down to the school. I went into the hall and saw I was the first one there. Gradually people began to arrive and I looked around. The boy I liked was nowhere in sight. I watched the hands of the clock creep toward eight o'clock, and just as I had completely given up hope, he came through the door of the hall. At exactly the same moment, my dad arrived to pick me up. I didn't bother to put up any resistance. I left quietly, unnoticed, and for the first time I resented skating and all that it entailed. I cried myself to sleep that night.

"Firebird," 1971

NINE

An Awesome Prospect

*I*N THE spring of 1970 I was training hard for the final test—the Gold. My parents were concerned about the time frame. Normally it takes a year to a year and a half to prepare for it, but we only had three months. Sonya felt strongly, however, that I must do it now. She wanted me to get as much experience as possible in Senior Competition before the 1972 Olympics.

There was one complication, however. Sonya was expecting a baby in May, around the same time as the Test. The question was, which would come first—the baby or the Test? I was living in New York for this period, this time with Nancy and Frank Streeter, another New York Skating Club family. Sonya came in four days a week to give me lessons. On the other days she coached me by phone. There I was at six in the morning—I would skate a school figure, walk off the ice, cross the rubber mats and pick up the telephone to give Sonya a report on how I had done. She would advise me and back I would go again. It was a bizarre situation. But when the time came I beat the baby, passed my Gold Test and moved into the world of Seniors.

That summer I went to Toronto again with Sonya and Peter. Peter choreographed my senior free skating program to Stravinsky's "Firebird." I knew from the minute we started that this was going to be a very special program for me. I felt a rapport with the music. Later Sonya prepared me for the Canadian Gold Test. It was more demanding than the U.S. Test, and Sonya thought it important that I get it. I spent hours training at the Cricket Club and finally the day of the test arrived.

I traced the paragraph loops well—they were the best I had ever done. They were so accurate, in fact, that at the point where I pulled out hard to change loops, I gouged a piece out of the ice. The next time I came around the circle my blade stuck in the deep gouge and I went flying. I was so embarrassed. I had never heard of anyone falling on a school figure before. But the judges didn't seem to be concerned. After consulting, they decided to let me pick up the figure from the point where I had fallen. I was so unnerved that I started the whole figure over again. Luckily I managed to avoid the rut on the second try, and I passed the test. I was now a fully qualified Senior in all aspects and all countries.

IN AUGUST I returned to Lake Placid to work with Mr. Lussi. Gordie was training there too, and we started to mirror skate together. Every time I put on the "Firebird" tape and started to skate my program, Gordie appeared out of nowhere, skating opposite me, matching every move and every gesture, in reverse.

I could never keep a straight face, and by the time we were finished, we would collapse in a heap on the ice, giggling. Officially, Mr. Lussi was not at all amused, but once or twice I thought I detected a faint smile playing around the corners of his mouth.

I turned fourteen in July and Gordie took me to see the movie *Oliver.* I sat through it twice and fell in love with Jack Wild who played the Artful Dodger. I daydreamed about him while I did patch. I thought about him while I walked to the rink in the early hours of the morning. I fantasized about him while I ate my supper, and I tried to dream about him at night. Finally I wrote him a letter explaining my feelings and suggesting he might like to write back. I drew small red flowers all around the edge of the envelope and sprayed some perfume inside. I waited eagerly for his reply, but it never came.

IN THE fall I started eighth grade and my mother and I took up our marathon schedule again. The only ice I could get now was at Skyrink from seven to nine A.M. and I couldn't give it up; I needed it to keep up my skating. And yet driving into New York City and back to Connecticut each morning, arriving well past first period, I missed so much English and math that I was falling farther and farther behind. Besides that, we were being worn ragged by the daily trip.

Finally Mom talked to Mrs. Long in New York. The room in her palatial apartment was still available if I could find a school in New York City. It seemed like the only sensible solution. That way I could fit my schooling around the available ice hours at the Skyrink and I could have the best of both worlds. My mom was as enthusiastic about the prospect as I was—no more tedious journeys on a daily basis. She, too, was tired of the endless highways and cold rinksides and was eager to find a way out of it.

A trail of suggestions led us to the Yoder School where I was immediately accepted. Yoder was a tutoring school, just suited to my needs at the time. The classes were small and it was easy to get to. I arranged to go to three hours of classes each morning. That way I could take advantage of the midday skating sessions.

My classmates were an intriguing group. All of them were there because for some reason or another they didn't fit into the normal school system. There was one boy who was very bright and wanted to be a surgeon. He was fifteen and already graduating from high school. He took me out one afternoon after school and bought me a silk rose from a street stand. I liked him. There was another kid who was going on nineteen and was as slow as the would-be surgeon was quick. It wasn't that he was stupid—he just didn't want to learn anything. He would sit at his desk doodling and staring into space. Then there was a very bright boy who couldn't carry on a conversation because as soon as anyone looked at him he would start to twitch and stutter.

There was one other girl my age, who chewed gum with great concentration. The first morning I was in class I noticed her leaning towards me, holding out a green package.

"Here," she offered, "want some gum?"

I shook my head, visions of Mr. Lussi looming up in front of me.

"Go on," she insisted.

I shook my head again and she withdrew, deeply offended. It took several weeks for me to overcome that initial setback, but eventually we did become friends.

With the pressures of commuting gone, I began to enjoy life much more. For one thing, I didn't have to get up so early, and that extra hour of sleep each morning was a wonderful luxury. It meant that, once in a while, I could stay up later at night. Sometimes the kids from Yoder would ask me to go to a movie with them, or else we'd hang out at a soda fountain, talking. I missed my family sometimes, but on the whole I was very happy living in New York City. I had almost begun to relax.

But by late fall the pressures started to build again. I was competing for the first time as a Senior Lady. I managed to qualify for the Nationals and that championship loomed ahead of me like a giant shadow. Although I knew that, as a first time Senior, I had little hope of making the World team, I could not ignore the possibility altogether. It was an awesome prospect.

AT CHRISTMAS I went to Lake Placid to work with Mr. Lussi again, and he was very pleased with the progress I had made at the Skyrink. One morning as I was doing jumps, he stood and watched, arms folded across his chest, brows knitted together. I did one jump after another, caught up in the sheer momentum and the speed. I loved to feel the cold wind rushing past me and to stroke very fast and feel

The Nationals, Buffalo, 1971

the edges. I thought it a wonderful thing to be able to control my body at that speed, to feel the force. It was exhilarating.

After a while Mr. Lussi called me over. "Dorothy," he said, glaring at me fiercely, "you are a speed demon. And that can be good if you have the right equipment."

I looked at him in surprise and then looked down at my skates.

"No—not the skates. You have very good skates. I mean the legs—the muscles. You weigh—what? A hundred pounds? But when you jump at high speeds that becomes two hundred pounds. You need a great deal of control and strength to be able to land such jumps and hold your edges."

He paused. "I believe in attacking jumps with total energy," he went on. "I believe in being bold and completely confident. It is the only way to jump. But you can never forget the momentum—the strength. You have to have very good thighs."

He walked away and I was left feeling as though I had somehow let him down. At the end of the rink, he turned. He shook his head slowly and smiled at me. "Such a jumper," he said. "I never knew a girl who jumped so big."

As the National Championships approached, I was scared to death. Suddenly I was going to be skating against Janet Lynn. I could hardly believe it. I was doing "Firebird" for my free program and Mom had the most beautiful dress made for me—brilliant red, with beads sewn on the back in the shape of butterfly wings. It was truly gorgeous.

The competition was in Buffalo, the scene of last year's disaster, but by the time I arrived I was feeling quite calm. Sonya had cautioned me not to expect too much my first year. "Just go for it," she said. "Have fun and enjoy yourself. This year you have nothing to lose."

In figures, my knees were shaking badly as I traced the loops in front of the judges. Somehow these judges all seemed much more forbidding than the judges from previous years. I squinted hard at the ice over my shoulder, trying to focus. In the end I placed eleventh and thought I had been lucky to finish as high as I did. I had no chance of winning, so I decided to enjoy the free skating section. Julie Holmes skated in front of me. She didn't skate particularly well—free style was not her strongest point—but her commanding lead in figures seemed to assure her of a place on the team going to the World Championships. Only Janet Lynn could hope to beat her.

Just before my turn to skate, Janet came over to me in the dressing room and held out her hand. "Good luck," she said. "I've watched you, and you're a very good free skater."

I floated on air out onto the ice and skated my heart out. I wasn't aware of the audience or the judges. I only thought of the blades and the music and the cool wind rushing past my face. I finished with a fast scratch spin and came to a halt facing the judges. Gradually my eyes began to focus again and I suddenly realized that people were standing up. The crowd was giving me a standing ovation. I came off the ice and waited for my marks. They were strong. With Janet still to skate, I was in first place in free skating. I was so happy. I hugged Sonya and Mom and Dad. Then I stood aside and watched Janet Lynn skate. She glided effortlessly across the ice, jumping in great fluid motions that seemed to defy gravity; spinning in such extraordinarily beautiful layback positions; sweeping around in long, flawless spirals, head high and a look akin to ecstasy on her face. I wanted to remember that performance all my life.

When the results were tabulated, I had finished fifth overall. But the biggest thrill was that I had finished second to Janet in free skating. That to me was very special.

In Good Hands

AFTER the Nationals, the gold and silver medalists—Janet Lynn and Julie Holmes—were to go to the North American Championships to compete against the Canadians. The third- and fourth-placed skaters had been invited to Sapporo, Japan, the following week to compete in the Pre-Olympic Championship. Julie declined the invitation to the North American Championships and was scheduled to go to Sapporo instead. Then that same day, the girl who had placed fourth in the Nationals announced her retirement from amateur competition.

Suddenly I was invited as fifth-place finisher to go to Japan with Julie Holmes. I would be representing the United States for the first time.

Julie brought her coach, Carlo Fassi, with her and, because I was so young, I got to bring my mom as a chaperon. For once we didn't have to consider the cost. This time the Olympic Fund paid for it all. Sonya came to see me off. "You'll be in good hands with Carlo," she told me. "He is one of the finest coaches in the world. He trained Peggy Fleming." I was terribly excited and a little overwhelmed by it all.

Pre-Olympics, Sapporo, Japan, 1971

Even compared to New York City, the streets of Tokyo were crowded and the traffic crazy. On our taxi ride from the airport, the driver was whipping through gas stations, cutting into oncoming lines of traffic and making U-turns to get ahead of the cars in front of him. Carlo—who had been to Japan several times before—kept up a running commentary on these proceedings and had us in stitches.

The Japanese treated us royally. Everything right down to the last detail was taken care of. The second day, Mom and I were the last ones to leave the arena and the manager of the ice rink offered to take us to his house for some refreshments. We accepted gladly and spent an interesting afternoon in a Japanese home. They spoke very little English so we all did a great deal of smiling and nodding. They served some strange delicacies made of green and red beans covered in sugar. After we had eaten, they gave us several beautiful dolls and fans to take home.

The figure segment of the competition was held on Thursday, and I was having such a good time that I forgot to be nervous. Suddenly I found myself once again squinting at the ice, tracing loops. I was not very successful—my tracings were a little shaky— but I finished third, right behind Julie Holmes and Carol Latham from Canada. There was one other Canadian girl and the rest of the competitors were Japanese. I hoped to make a better showing in the free skating.

The stands were full on the night of the free skating. When I went out on the ice a loud cheer went up. I had been told that Japanese audiences rarely cheer, so I was very surprised. Later I found out that Japanese television had done a program about me, showing me in my "Firebird" dress and calling me "The Little Princess," and that several magazines had run cover stories on me. As I started to skate—to "Firebird" again—I was elated

The Head jacket arriving in Japan

"Firebird" in Japan

and skated a good strong program. Julie was the last to skate and gave a very solid performance. She took the gold medal and I—to my surprise—took the silver.

Right after Sapporo, we were flown to Tokyo to skate for Crown Prince Takeda at a rink in a modern shopping mall. It was a public performance and when it was all over the Prince came down and presented each of us with a beautiful string of pearls. The press followed me everywhere, taking photographs. I was to remain in the Japanese public eye right through the Winter Olympics a year later.

THE MOST IMPORTANT thing to come out of the Japanese trip—apart from the experience of competing internationally—was meeting Carlo Fassi. By the time we arrived back in the United States, he had voiced an interest in working with me. "I don't take students without a great deal of faith in their ability," he told Mom. "Dorothy is a very good skater—I could be very helpful to her in many ways. Especially with her school figures—they are still weak."

We knew he was right. My figures were always letting me down. Mom promised to be in touch with him.

Carlo was very important politically in the skating world. Although we knew very little about the inner workings of international skating in those days, we knew enough to be in awe of Carlo Fassi. There were many who believed that without Carlo, a skater could never achieve any stature in world competition. My mother was not swayed by mass opinion, but the fact was she liked Carlo enormously. We were also impressed by his track record—he had trained many great skaters, including Peggy Fleming at the time she won the 1968 Olympics. Finally, he specialized in school figures, my weakest point. All this persuaded

With Bill and my souvenirs from Japan, and right, the silver medal.

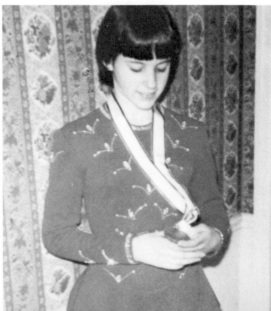

my parents to send me to Tulsa for the summer to train with Carlo and see how we got along.

BEFORE I LEFT for Tulsa, I went up to Wellesley to visit Bill and Jonsie. I had been so busy that I had seen very little of them the previous two years. There was always some reason why I couldn't go—training, exhibiting, competing. I never seemed to have any free time. But suddenly I was seized with a sense of urgency which propelled me onto a train and back to the house by the pond.

It was as I remembered it, and I drew great comfort from that. But after dinner, as I sat sipping my coffee (I no longer took sugar, but didn't have the heart to tell Jonsie), I saw how the two of them had aged. They were sitting close together by the fire. As I watched the firelight playing across the two creased, worn faces, I was filled with a great surge of love. Their eyes were the same, but I noticed how tired they seemed now. I had an intense sense of the passing of time and for a moment, I also felt panic. The momentum of my life controlled me as if I were being swept along in a strong current. The only way I could swim ashore would be to give up skating altogether, and yet I knew that I couldn't do that. It just seemed sometimes that the price was high.

I FLEW INTO Tulsa, Oklahoma, in late May and was met by Carlo's wife, Christa. I was going to stay with them and be a part of their family. For the first time I could remember, neither of my parents planned to visit me during my training. I felt curiously relieved.

In many ways the Fassi's were the First Family of skating. They lived in a large modern apartment on the outskirts of Tulsa, about five miles from the ice rink. Christa was a fantastic homemaker. She kept the apartment spotless, yet everyone who came to visit felt very comfortable and welcome. Christa seemed to me the ideal woman—elegant, beautiful and very talented. She spoke with a soft German accent and I idolized her. The Fassi's had two beautiful young children—a son, Ricky and a daughter, Monika. I quickly became a member of the family, and I loved being there with them all.

Carlo had excellent ice time available to him but I still had to get up early for patch. I would come down for breakfast at six A.M. and make myself some cold cereal and toast. Christa would make a pot of coffee and when Carlo came down at six-twenty he would pour a cup, drink it standing up and ask me if I was ready to leave. He did everything very fast and would already be halfway out the door by the time I answered. I had the patch at the far end of the rink where from seven to eleven I engaged in my usual method of getting through the tedious hours of figure practice: I fantasized. At noon we drove back to the house for lunch. Carlo radiated energy and would be full of amusing anecdotes about people in the skating world. Before lunch was over I always had a stitch in my side from laughing. The rest of the day was given over to free skating and those were the hours I loved best. It was such a release to race around the rink, spinning and jumping, narrowly missing other people and impatiently waiting for my turn to use the tape deck.

At four Christa and the children picked me up and we went to the store for supplies—food disappeared like magic in that household. At six Carlo came home. Gone was the energy of the morning. Instead he collapsed into his chair in front of the television and watched the evening news. Then he read his Italian newspaper, ate dinner and kissed the children good-night. He rarely spoke at those times except in perfunctory sentences. He was exhausted.

Carlo began to work on my figures. He had an uncanny knack for teaching them. He rarely dwelt on small, individual details, preferring to deal with the total performance—the overall look of the skater. "No one thing is more important than the other," he said emphatically. "It's all important."

Carlo himself had been a World medalist back in 1953, recognized for his solid technique rather than his free skating. When he went into teaching he built a reputation that no other trainer in the world has ever been able to equal. He spares no effort to produce the best all-round skater he can, which is probably the reason he has more Olympic champions than any other trainer. He sends his students to the best outside sources he can find for choreography and free skating. He is wise enough to know that the better his student looks, the more credit he will get. Unlike other, less secure trainers, Carlo is not afraid of losing his students. I don't think the possibility even occurs to him.

I had been in Tulsa about a week when I began to make friends with the other skaters at the rink. It was so different from the hostile atmosphere at the Skyrink. We hung out together at the snack bar between patches and I grew to feel like a member of the group. We talked and laughed and teased one another; I felt happier than at any time I could remember. These were friends I didn't have to pretend with—they were seasoned skaters, and they understood everything.

Carlo was able to tune in to his students' moods. He had an instinct for knowing how to handle each one of us. If we were just being lazy he showed no mercy. "What do you think you're doing?" he would shout. "This is ridiculous." But if we were truly upset, or unable to get anything accomplished, he would send us away. "Go on home," he would say kindly. "You're doing no good here today."

Sometimes, when I just couldn't seem to get a jump right, Carlo would come over and shout at me. "Hey! Are you crazy—you're going to kill yourself like that." Then he would explain to me that I was holding back—hesitating. "You can't keep anything back," he said. "You have to believe you can do it or you never will. You have to put everything into it."

One morning I was tracing a figure when I saw Carlo watching me intently. Finally he called me off the ice and asked me what I thought I was doing. I looked at him blankly. "Tracing figures," I said.

"But what were you *thinking* about?" he persisted. "It wasn't the figures."

"I—I was thinking about the movie I saw last night," I stammered.

He made a gesture of impatience. "Hey," he said, "if you are going to do good figures, you don't ever *think* while you are skating. You make the mind a blank. You think only of the blade on the ice. Okay?"

It wasn't okay. I told him I didn't think that I could get through these sessions if I couldn't daydream. It would be too boring.

He drew in his breath. "Then give it up, Dorothy. Just give it up. Either you do it right, or you don't do it at all—okay?"

"Okay," I said finally. This was obviously lesson number one—be total. I decided to give it a try.

ELEVEN

First You Skate, Then You Die

$\mathcal{M}$Y STAY in Tulsa was interrupted by the United States Figure Skating Association—they chose me to represent the U.S. in the St. Gervais Championship in France, and in the Nebelhorn Trophy in Oberstdorf, Germany, a week later. Juli McKinstry was to go as my teammate. She told me these competitions were important training ground for international competitors. The U.S.F. S.A. was preparing us for the time when we might be on the World team.

Mom and Dad and Marcia all decided to come with me to Europe. None of us had ever been there before, so we were all very excited about the trip. Since my parents could only stay for the first week, Marcia was to act as my chaperon for the Nebelhorn Trophy. She was only sixteen and I was still fourteen. What fun we would have on our own! The night before we left, I lay awake for hours thinking about castles on the Rhine and flaxen-haired boys in Lederhosen.

"And the chocolate," Marcia murmured, drifting off to sleep. "Don't forget the chocolate."

The St. Gervais Championship was first. When we arrived the team leader gave us some instructions. "Don't drink the

St. Gervais, France, 1971

water," he warned. "And be careful for the first three days or so—the altitude is very high and it can make you sick unless you give yourself time to adjust." The advice went in one ear and out the other. Juli McKinstry and I were sharing a room, so we rushed upstairs, dumped our bags and spent the whole day exploring the quaint old cobbled streets of St. Gervais.

The school figures segment of the competition had two separate phases spread over two days. The first day we did three figures and by the time we both had finished Juli and I had throbbing heads. We felt terrible. Back in our room Mom made us take aspirin. We threw up. Mom thought it might be a nervous reaction to the competition and made us get into bed. We slept fitfully all afternoon and by the early evening, Juli was much better. I, however, was worse. I was running a high fever and was delirious. I began to babble. At some point during the evening Marcia came to visit, but I have no memory of it.

Carlo, arriving just in time for the second day of figures, brought chicken soup and I opened my eyes to see him standing over me with a small, steaming bowl. "Eat," he commanded. "You've been talking crazy."

I managed to keep the soup down and finally I slept. By the next morning I felt much better. Even though I was weak there was no question that I would skate the three remaining figures. There is a universal rule in skating—"First you skate, then you die."

By the time free skating came around I was back to full strength. I managed to eat a hearty breakfast and skate better than I had expected. When the results were posted I found I had won. I was elated. I ran to my room to phone Sonya with the good news.

Her voice came across the Atlantic. "Good, Dorothy! I knew you could do it. I'm very proud of you."

Victory at St. Gervais, with Juli McKinstry, left, and Julie Black of Canada

"I wish you were here," I said.

"Dorothy," Sonya said quietly, "Carlo is there. He is your coach now. You are very fortunate to have him."

Carlo left after St. Gervais and my parents drove Marcia and me through the Alps in a little rented car. I shall never forget that journey. Mile after mile of breathtaking scenery, all in vivid colors. In Oberstdorf my parents settled us into the hotel and left. Dad's vacation was over. Marcia and I fell in love with the little village. It was picture-postcard perfect. The hotel surrounded the ice rink on three sides, and the ice sparkled under the bluest of skies. The dining room, which became our constant haunt, overlooked the ice.

The first morning of school figures, I went down for breakfast in my figure costume and brought my skates so I would be ready when my turn came. While eating, I became engrossed in a conversation with David Santee, a U.S. team member who would later become a World silver medalist. We were so busy exchanging funny stories and jokes that I forgot the competition altogether.

Suddenly one of the officials came flying into the room calling my name frantically. "You're next," she shouted. "I've been looking everywhere for you."

Crossly she grabbed me by the hand and dragged me down the stairs puffing and panting. I barely had time to pull on my skates and lace them up before the judges called my name. Just after I finished, I noticed I was wearing my sweater inside out.

Oberstdorf is famous for its chocolate and Marcia and I ate chocolate everything. We ate it in cakes, in bars, in candies, in desserts and in huge bowls as fondue. I loved nothing better than to dip chunks of fruit into the bubbling milk chocolate and watch the thick liquid drip off the end of my fork. We looked in all the shops and bought brightly colored dirndl skirts and puffy-sleeved blouses. I bought a music box for Jonsie and a wonderful carved pipe for Bill, although he didn't smoke. I sent postcards to everyone I could think of, including Jack Wild, my *Oliver* heartthrob. I hadn't really forgiven him for not answering my letter the year before, but I thought I would have one more try.

"I am here competing in the Nebelhorn Trophy," I wrote.

Marcia read it over my shoulder. "He'll think you're a mountaineer," she said. But I sent it anyway.

The free skating was on Friday. I put on my red "Firebird" dress, brushed my hair and went down to the dining room to wait. The frantic official was waiting for me. "You missed your turn to skate," she said accusingly. "You drew number one." My heart sank. "However, I've arranged for you to skate later." She looked at me with a small, strained smile. I could breathe again.

I won the Nebelhorn Trophy, and that summer my sister and I became friends. On the way to the airport she handed me a small black box.

"It's not your birthday," she said. "But I think you'd better have it now."

Inside the box was a beautiful Swiss watch.

BY THE FALL of 1971 I had skated in four major competitions—Buffalo, Sapporo, St. Gervais and Oberstdorf. In many ways I suppose my first year in Senior Ladies' had been a big success. It hadn't been easy—there were many moments when I felt discouraged. But through all the ups and downs, I had never had a single doubt about what I wanted to do. I knew there was a lot more hard work still ahead—I was now competing against skaters who had years more experience and training—but I was prepared for that. I wanted so badly to be the National Champion.

In Tulsa Carlo started training me in earnest. He would stand beside my patch and yell, "You're a dummy, Dorothy! What are you doing?" Over and over he would make me trace those figures, waving his arms in exasperation, pointing to my circles. "That's ridiculous!" he shouted. "Ridiculous!" I'd try again, but he would stop me. "Hey! Don't you know these figures yet? Why are you being so stupid?" I'd peer at the ice, trying to see the tracing. "Can't you *see* that?" Carlo demanded. And I would stamp my feet and kick the ice in frustration. Thinking I was being fresh, Carlo would send me home. "Get out of here," he'd say. And Christa would come and pick me up and dry my tears.

I went to a wonderful private school called Holland House that summer. It was my first really pleasant school experience. I took creative writing and math, trying to make up for some of the work I had missed during the year. I made up my mind that I wanted to stay with Carlo. Even though he seemed to be always frustrated with me, I felt I was learning some very important things. And I was also very happy.

In the summer Carlo decided to move to Lake Placid to teach. I sat in the front seat of the car as we drove across the country and tried to navigate. We were approaching an exit somewhere in Iowa when Carlo said, "What number is that exit?"

I squinted hard, trying to read the sign. "I don't know."

"What do you mean, you don't know?"

"I can't read it," I answered miserably.

We came towards another exit. "What does that say, Dorothy?" he asked.

I tried again but we were almost at the turnoff before I could read it clearly.

"You are blind," Carlo said. "No wonder you can't see your figures." He said no more about it until we were in Lake Placid, where he telephoned my parents. I went to Connecticut a week later and had my eyes examined. The doctor told me I should be wearing glasses all the time.

"She needs big frames," Carlo told the optician. "They must come down to the cheeks, so . . . Must be *very* big, okay? That way she sees out the corners to do the figures."

The optician looked puzzled but did as he was told and made

me a very large pair of glasses. Those frames, born out of sheer necessity, were later to become my trademark and a fashion trend. But all I cared about was that at last I could see. My whole world changed. I found I had been walking around in a fuzzy half-world for years. Suddenly colors seemed brighter, objects became sharper and I could see small details I hadn't even known existed. Even my figures improved.

LATER IN THE summer Carlo sent me to Toronto to work on my free skating with Ellen Burka. I met Mrs. Burka the first morning I was there. I was immediately drawn to this large, warm-hearted woman dressed in a gigantic red topcoat and woolen mittens. She had curly blonde hair and peered through her spectacles at us with an air of mild surprise.

"I won't have anyone in my class who isn't prepared to work hard," she told us. She looked around the group challengingly and since no one dared to answer her, she continued. "We are going to start with stroking classes."

Loud groans came from the group and she glowered at us. "All right," she said firmly. "Since you seem to feel you are already perfect at stroking, let us see. Dorothy Hamill, you will begin."

I, like all the other students, failed Mrs. Burka's stroking test. Stroking, she told us, is not the simple movement it would appear to be. It is the absolute basis of all skating. Generally, she told us, her eyes boring into us, stroking is not taught correctly. This summer we were going to learn to stroke properly.

So we began. She taught us to stroke—both forward and backward—using long, smooth edges. She taught us to carry our heads high and to use our arms properly. And somehow she also managed to turn what might have been a boring exercise into something we all looked forward to and enjoyed.

Ellen Burka had been the Dutch Champion in 1945–46. Then she had emigrated to Canada where she began to teach skating. When her daughter Petra won the 1965 World Championship, Mrs. Burka's position in the skating world became firmly established. She would later train many champions, including Toller Cranston, the legendary Canadian skater.

Mrs. Burka gave us theater-on-ice classes every Wednesday evening. We were given a story line or a role to play and, besides skating well, we were also asked to mime to the music. She taught me so many things about performing—about becoming a character, about climbing inside of your music so that it surrounds you like walls, and about projecting to an audience without losing the emotional focus of your performance. I loved these classes and I tried very hard to take everything in.

Mrs. Burka worked with me privately on my free skating. She was determined that I would leave Toronto with a consistent double axel. Over and over again she would make me do them, forcing me to concentrate. "Hold that landing," she would shout. "Hold it longer—*Longer!*"

She wouldn't let up. "Do it again," she ordered. "Get your head up—*Up!*"

Finally I snapped. "It *is* up!" I yelled back at her. "It won't go any higher."

But she wouldn't accept excuses. No matter how much I complained or kicked the ice or swore under my breath, she kept right on drilling me. And the truth was that I liked to be trained that way. I liked that kind of discipline, and by the end of the summer I had a consistent double axel and great stroking edges.

THE DAY BEFORE I left Toronto, a jumbo jet went down near the airport killing everyone on board, and when I got to the airport the next day to go back to Lake Placid I was suddenly afraid to fly. The plane to Lake Placid was a little Allegheny crop duster, and by the time I got on board and sat down in my seat, my mouth was dry and my

Labor Day show, Lake Placid, 1972

palms were sweating. I kept telling myself that this was ridiculous. The statistics were all in favor of air travel—much safer than cars. But all I could think about was the Air Canada crash. I clutched the arms of my seat until my knuckles showed white. I promised God I'd do all sorts of things if only I could arrive safely in Lake Placid. When we took off, I screwed my eyes shut so tightly that when I opened them again all I could see were little colored spots. Outside the plane window there was nothing but dense, grey clouds. We bumped and jolted our way through them, with the tail section swinging wildly. I knew this was the end. The engine began to make a funny noise. Why didn't the pilot say something to us? He must know we were all scared to death. Why didn't he speak to us in a nice calm voice and assure us that we were going to land safely in Lake Placid?

Finally the drinks came around and I managed to get a rum and orange. The stewardess didn't even ask how old I was. I drank it down in one gulp and closed my eyes. "Please, God, keep us safe," I prayed. And in the end He did, because twenty minutes later we landed safely, if somewhat precariously.

My mother came to Lake Placid in the fall and we got an apartment. Looking back, I just don't know how we could have survived a whole winter in that dark, dingy place. All we had was one tiny room in an old house—it wasn't even a nice old house. It was damp and cold and had room for only two single beds and a table. We shared a bathroom down the hall with the other four tenants. I hated it.

Not everything about Lake Placid was grim, however. The school officials were used to skaters and arranged the school schedule around our ice time. It was a welcome change from the years of disapproving teachers.

At the rink I worked harder than ever. Carlo told me that if I could improve my figures I might just have a chance to make the Olympic team. I longed to go back to Sapporo, and I focused on that goal as I trained. I did push-ups and stretching exercises; I jogged around the lake. When every muscle in my body hurt I knew I was beginning to make progress.

I won both the North Atlantics and Easterns and I felt my confidence growing. Mom and I went home to Connecticut for Christmas and for the first time I was restless there. I wanted to get back to Lake Placid and start training again.

We returned the day after Christmas. My friend David, the boy who ran the concession stand, was home for the vacation and I spent a lot of time talking to him. Mom and Carlo seemed upset by this. I guess they were afraid he was distracting me— and maybe he was—and they were both very hostile to him. One evening David came to the rink to watch me skate. While the ice was being resurfaced, he sat with me, his arm draped around my shoulders. He had a terrible cold. I saw Mom and Carlo talking and eventually Carlo came over to us. He told David to go away and leave me alone. David stared at Carlo for a moment, then he got up and quietly left the arena. I burst into tears.

I didn't see David for several days after that. I missed him terribly, and my eyes were red from crying. He was so important to me at that time—a real friend who wasn't part of the skating world. Someone I could confide in.

Carlo was pushing me very hard. He had to leave for Italy and wanted to be certain I was training properly before he left. I jogged and stretched until I hurt all over. I did push-ups and deep breathing and I increased my on-ice training. I tried hard not to think about the Nationals in Long Beach, California— they were only four weeks away.

Then, on New Year's Eve, disaster struck. David called me and asked if we could talk. He suggested we meet by the lake and go for a walk. I had been feeling under the weather all day but forgot all about that at the prospect of seeing David again. I pulled on my warmest clothes and ran out the door.

By the time I reached the lake I knew something was wrong with me. My feet dragged like lead weights and waves of nausea kept sweeping through me. I was shivering uncontrollably in spite of my pile-lined coat. My head felt as though it was too heavy for my neck to support, and my eyes burned with fever. David took one look at me and told me he was taking me straight home. We would talk later.

Mom put me to bed, and although she covered me with three thick blankets, my teeth would not stop chattering. I couldn't eat at all. The doctor came and told Mom I had the Asian flu. I was to stay in bed for the next few days; he would come to see me again. The National Championships were rapidly approaching and I was too weak even to stand up.

When I got a little better the doctor suggested I bundle up and go out to skate. I would work the flu off in no time, he said. I felt all right as I went down to the rink—wobbly, but all right. I had lost ten pounds, and even though I was sick, I wasn't too sick to be aware of how good that must look.

I had skated for almost an hour when I became violently ill again. By evening my temperature was over 104° and I had become delirious. The doctor told my mother not to worry, gave me a shot and left her a prescription. I lay in bed for another week without eating. Altogether I lost fourteen pounds. I had never been so ill.

Finally I got up because I knew Nationals were only two weeks away and I was determined to be there. I was painfully thin. My clothes hung off me and my legs trembled when I tried to stand. I developed cravings for foods that I normally never ate—peanut butter and milk shakes. I couldn't get enough of them. I went back onto the ice and I skated. At first I could only do an hour—but gradually I increased the time to my normal routine. I was weak but felt a kind of euphoria.

When Carlo came back and saw how skinny I was he seemed shocked. He made me eat lots of whole grain and wheat germ. Normally I had to be careful of eating too much starch, but now I couldn't swallow enough of it. In spite of everything, Carlo said he was pleased to see me skating so well and felt I still had a chance to make the Olympic team. He made me spend extra time on my figures. Christa came to the rink and watched over me like a mother hen.

WHEN WE ARRIVED in Long Beach the atmosphere was charged with electricity. Everyone was aware the Winter Olympics was only three weeks away. Carlo was pleased when I placed fifth in school figures. He told me that if I free skated well I could pull to third and make the team. I was filled with a wild kind of hope. Although I was still frail I had never in all my life felt better about my skating. It was one of those rare times when you feel like you can't make a mistake. In the free skating everything was on—I caught every beat of the music, landed every jump clean, spun on a dime and managed the footwork without a hitch. When I finished my program, I knew I had done my very best. Carlo hugged me and told me I was a good girl. I waited for the results, hardly daring to look.

When they came, they were devastating. The judges had given me low marks. Tears came and I tried hard to hide them. I can't remember, through all the competitions I skated as an amateur, ever being more disappointed.

Skating for Janet Lynn, 1972

Back in the dressing room I clung to Carlo, sobbing. "I thought I would make third," I cried. "I wanted so badly to be on the Olympic team." Carlo dried my tears and lifted my chin with his big hand.

"Hey!" he said. "You skated excellent. You did the best you could. Don't cry anymore, okay?"

Eventually I stopped crying and went out to watch Janet Lynn skate the winning performance. I forgot my own disappointment as she moved across the ice with such grace. I wished with all my heart that she could win the Olympic gold medal. When the final marks were tabulated for the Ladies' Singles I had placed fourth, a fraction behind Suna Murray, who had come in third and therefore made the Olympic team.

I thought I had handled my disappointment well until I had to go for a fitting for an Olympic team uniform. It was a precaution in case one of the others should drop out. But all the time I knew that I wouldn't be going and misery lodged in my throat like a big lump. I couldn't swallow.

Later my parents took me to Disneyland and I wept my way through the Enchanted Forest and sobbed miserably at the antics of Goofy and Donald. We gave up and went home. I cried for a whole week. I couldn't stop. It was like the end of the world for me—I had this great, empty feeling that refused to go away. Every time I looked in a magazine or turned on the television there would be something there to remind me of the Olympics in Sapporo. People tried to cheer me up, telling me how young I was and how I would be there in 1976 for sure, but it didn't help. I couldn't think that far ahead. When I want something, I want it now. I guess I've always been that way.

LYN MALONE

TWELVE

The Main Event

$\mathcal{B}$EFORE he left for the Olympics Carlo warned me to keep on skating hard. "Train," he warned. "Keep busy, okay?"

My mother took me to Toronto to have some new exhibition numbers choreographed by Osborne Colson. I had been invited to exhibit at the F.I.S.U. Games in Lake Placid, an international sports festival with representatives from many different fields. It was difficult to get going after all that had happened, but I remembered Carlo's advice and tried to work hard.

The night I skated the exhibition in Lake Placid Carlo called from Japan to say that Julie Holmes, the National silver medalist, had quit skating. She had placed fourth in Olympics and chose not to go on to Worlds, which were in Calgary, Canada, only two weeks later.

"I want you to go to Calgary, Dorothy," Carlo told me. "You will take Julie's place on the team."

I stood there at the phone with my mouth open. I didn't believe him. Surely Julie would change her mind. But she didn't and I found myself sitting beside my mother on a plane to Calgary.

I had no thoughts of winning a medal at the Worlds—none

Skyrink, New York City, 1973

at all. I was just very happy to be there. I had never seen a
World Championship, let alone competed in one. Still, I felt
very uncomfortable among the other competitors. Most of them
had been on World teams before and they all seemed to know
each other. Gordie McKellen was the only one I knew, and he
was too preoccupied to speak to me very much. I felt terribly
out of place, but I walked around with what I hoped was a smile
on my face and tried to look relaxed. Inside I was desperately
lonely.

Still, it was exciting to see all the famous foreign skaters.
Karen Magnussen from Canada (the local girl); Beatrix Schuba,
the girl from Austria who was said to have the best figures in
the history of skating; little Christine Errath from East Germany
and her teammate Sonja Morgenstern. There were skaters from
all over the world. I watched the other girls in the dressing
room and thought how amazing it was that I was here in the
same competition as these great champions. I didn't even try to
make friends that first year—I just tried to memorize all the
faces and names and take everything in.

Carlo tried to help me with my figures, but on the morning
of the figures competition I was a mess. My knees were shaking
so badly that my circles were uneven and my tracings were all
over the place. I placed ninth in school figures.

The Men's final was before ours, so I watched with great
interest. Of course I was rooting for Gordie McKellen and John
Misha Petkevich but it was not their year. I was especially sad
for John Misha. I knew it was to be his last year in competition.
He had decided to pursue an academic career. A Harvard under-
graduate, he was later to be awarded a Rhodes scholarship to
Oxford. The Eastern bloc countries made a clean sweep of the
medals. The gold went to Ondrej Nepala from Czechoslovakia.
The Soviet skater Vladimir Kovalev took third place, and I

admired his distinct freestyle skating. I also remember Jan Hoffman, who was in his first year of international competition. This tiny German skater was to later win several World titles.

The Ladies' free skating was on Saturday night. I changed into my "Firebird" costume, took several deep breaths and went out to skate. I think I did quite well—at least I have no memory of making any major mistakes. Afterwards I sighed with relief and sat back to watch the other competitors. Janet Lynn, as always, skated beautifully to take the bronze medal. Beatrix Schuba had built up such a commanding lead in figures that she was just able to edge Karen Magnussen out of the gold medal. I finished fifth in the free skating and seventh overall. I was completely taken by surprise. My other teammate, Suna Murray, who had beaten me out of third place in Nationals, finished in eighth position.

Back in Lake Placid I went to work on my figures and thought about Beatrix Schuba. She was a heavily built girl with little aptitude for free skating, yet she skated the most incredible figures. She could trace circles one on top of the other and never vary an inch. Janet Lynn, on the other hand, had to struggle with her figures and only shone when she was free skating. I wondered how meaningful it was to pitch these two skaters—both outstanding in their own fields—against one another. Who is to say which one is better when they are both so different? The physical build of a great figure skater is distinct from that of a great free skater. The edges for school figures are quite different from those used for free skating. It would seem to make more sense for the two categories to be entirely separated. John Curry, Janet Lynn, Melissa Militano and Toller Cranston all have great free skating edges but, of those four, only John Curry has great figure edges too. And John is the only one of them ever to have won a World Championship.

CARLO MOVED his teaching practice to Colorado that spring. His stay in Lake Placid had been only temporary while he was waiting for his own ice rink to open in Denver. My parents decided that, even though it meant going much farther away from home, Mom and I should follow him down there. It wouldn't be wise to change trainers at this point. Mom rented another dingy little apartment on the outskirts of town. It was all she could afford and we made the best of it. Dad, of course, had to stay behind in Connecticut with Marcia. It was hard for Mom, being separated from Dad like that, but she had made up her mind to do whatever was necessary. The only time she complained was when I threw a tantrum at the rink. Then I would have to go back to the apartment and listen to a lecture on commitment.

In the summer I was picked to represent the United States at the Richmond Trophy in London, England. Lynn Nightingale was representing Canada and skated right before me. In the middle of her performance a big piece of the arena roof fell onto the ice, missing Lynn by inches. The event was stopped while the roof was examined. It was two hours before the officials decided it was safe to go on with the competition. Lynn skated her number over again but was clearly shaken by the experience. I was a little tense during my performance, half expecting to hear a crash on the ice at any moment, but in the end I finished in first place.

At the end of that week I was invited to perform for Her Majesty, Queen Elizabeth, at a gala BBC televised ice show. I decided to get my hair cut for the occasion. I had read that the stylist who cut Julie Andrews hair for *The Sound of Music* had a salon in Oxford Street. I sought him out and persuaded him to cut my hair. An hour later I was standing outside of Harrod's, crying as I looked at my reflection in the window. It wasn't Julie

Andrews I saw but Dorothy Hamill with very short hair sticking out in all directions. It was a mess, and I wished the earth would open and swallow me. But in the end I skated for the Queen, and my hair didn't seem to shock her too badly, for she was kind enough to tell me how much she had enjoyed my performance.

A week later my father and I flew to Czechoslovakia where I was to compete in Skate Prague. We spent many hours exploring that beautiful city. One evening, quite by chance, we came across a street named after Jackson Haines, the great nineteenth century American skater.

Skate Prague was of historical importance because it was the first competition to introduce the compulsory short program. This phase was added in order to bridge the gap between the good figure skaters and the good free skaters. It is worth twenty percent of the total mark and requires a skater to execute seven compulsory moves during a two minute program. It was an addition I welcomed at Prague, and I won not only the short program, but also the Prague Trophy.

My dad had invited me to go to Vienna after Skate Prague. We booked a flight that went via Bratislava, Czechoslovakia, where the 1973 World Championships were to be held. We planned to take a taxi to the arena and have a quick look at it before going on to Vienna.

Czechoslovakia was our first experience behind the Iron Curtain and we were more than a little nervous. In Bratislava nobody spoke English. We attracted a great deal of attention as we waved our arms about, trying to explain that we needed a cab to go to the ice arena. Finally we made a deal with someone who had a private car, and we were driven at top speed through gray suburbs and cobble streets. Police seemed to be everywhere. Dad was sure we were under surveillance. At the stadium, Dad was so scared that the car would drive off without us that he made me wait while he looked at the arena. I was petrified. When we realized that we had missed the last flight of the day out of Bratislava, we asked the driver to take us to the train station. We didn't intend to spend a night there. At the station the driver refused the American dollars Dad offered him. Usually this money is eagerly accepted, but not this time. Once again I was left as security until Dad came back with local currency.

The train ride was terrible. We were five people deep in tiny, cramped carriages, and the air was stifling. We rattled through the night until we reached the border where the train shuddered to a halt. Eventually police came on board with dogs. They took our passports and went away. Dad and I looked at each other—there we were, in the middle of the night, on a train behind the Iron Curtain and we had no passports. But in the end the police returned the passports and we were allowed to proceed.

Vienna was wonderful. I shall never forget those few days there, walking around the streets looking at all the landmarks and absorbing the aura of its great musical heritage. We stayed at the Imperial Hotel, which was elegant and romantic. I felt totally at home in Vienna, and I vowed to return to that lovely city as soon as possible.

AT THE END of summer, my mother and I returned to Denver. Carlo was already looking ahead to the 1973 World Championships and stepped up my training schedule. I knew how important it was, but I began to feel more and more like a robot as I pushed myself through the sessions, not daring to stop and analyze how I felt about what I was doing. Suppose I were to discover I was unhappy—what then? So I didn't question. I just went from day to day, carrying out Carlo's instructions. He would stand at the edge of my patch chanting his litany, *A figure skater does not think. A figure skater does not think.* But I *did* think—I couldn't stop. I traced my figures and dreamed about Vienna, trying to look as though my mind were blank. If Carlo wasn't fooled he never said so, because eventually he would nod his head and go away.

It seemed I was always the first one in the rink in the morning and the last one to leave at night. I had made an important discovery that winter: it took me twice as long to learn something new as it seemed to take other skaters, and even then I had to work hard to keep everything together. Free skating was no longer the carefree thing it had once been. Carlo would put me through punishing workouts. Double axel, double lutz, more double axels. Over and over again. Down I would go, crashing onto the ice time after time, but I had to get up and do it all over again no matter how much my hips hurt or how bruised my thighs were. Usually by the end of the morning session I would have everything just right and Carlo would dismiss me with a smile. I would go off for lunch filled with a false sense of security.

In the evening I would go back for three more hours of work and would start falling on the same jumps I had done perfectly that morning. I got so discouraged. Carlo stood there drilling it all into my head until finally I would burst into tears, shout at him and rush off the ice.

One night Carlo came after me and sat down beside me. "Dorothy," he said, "you do this to yourself. It's all in your head. You can do those jumps perfectly well, but you are talking yourself out of them before you even take off. You are bound to fall."

I knew he was right. I remembered Gus Lussi's statement, "The moment you hesitate, it's all over. You've lost it." I went back out and for a while everything was all right—until I forgot again and started to hesitate.

One morning, just before Christmas, I was especially tired and had missed the early session. I went right out and started into the jumps. My body wasn't warmed up, so the first time I fell I felt something tear in the back of my leg. I hobbled off the ice. Carlo looked at it and told me I had pulled a muscle. He bandaged it for me and told me to stay off it for a few days so it would have a chance to heal. We were only four weeks away from the Nationals in Minneapolis.

Warming up is so important to a skater. Usually I am a stickler for it. I don't feel comfortable until I'm really huffing and puffing and can feel my blood and my heart pounding. Just like a racehorse, you have to warm up at the beginning—before you perform—and warm down again after. For me spinning is the best way to warm up. Gus Lussi always told me that if you spin for ten minutes you are ready to start jumping. In any case, you are never ready to jump until you're warm enough to take your sweater off. The pulled muscle healed quickly enough, but it taught me a lesson.

I had other troubles that winter. I developed a serious complex about figures. I began to joke about them—"Oh, my figures are so rotten they look like modern art." I was so convinced that I couldn't do them that when I went to skate in competitions my knees would shake and my foot would shake and I would wobble all over the place. Carlo was at his wits end. "You're a disaster," he said in despair.

At the 1973 Nationals, my figures ruined any chance I had for the gold. But free skating was a different matter. I pulled right up to second place behind Janet Lynn. In one way, I would have liked to beat her, but at the same time I was glad I hadn't. It wouldn't have seemed right.

Second to Janet Lynn, U.S. Nationals, 1973, with Juli McKinstry, right

As I stood on the winner's podium next to Janet, I thought I had never been happier in my life. I was a Senior Ladies' medalist at the age of sixteen and I was going to the Worlds in Bratislava as Janet Lynn's teammate. It was enough for now.

THIRTEEN

The Butterflies of Hope

$\mathcal{B}$RATISLAVA was my second World Championship. Just before I left Denver for Czechoslovakia, Doris Fleming (Peggy's mother) gave me a hundred dollars. "This is not for skating," she told me. "This is for you, Dorothy. Buy yourself something pretty with it." Mrs. Fleming had helped see me through my Asian flu the year before and had always supported and encouraged me. She seemed to know just what to do at any given moment, and her gift meant a lot to me.

At Bratislava, the Czech Ondrej Nepala won the Men's gold medal, and the crowd went wild. I had never heard a response so enthusiastic, and so deafening. Jan Hoffman—the little East German skater I had first encountered at the Calgary Worlds the year before—surprised us all by finishing in third place.

Carlo, who had an uncanny knack of predicting results, told me that if nothing went wrong I would finish in fifth position in the Ladies' event. He also said that first place should go to Janet Lynn. I finished, as he had forecast, in fifth place. Janet did not fare so well. Knowing this was to be her last attempt to win a World title, she skated passionately and many of us had tears in our eyes as we watched this great lady of the ice trying once again to take her rightful place in skating history. But

Spinning—10 revolutions per second,
almost 60 miles an hour

Janet fell twice and those mistakes robbed her of first place. She finished second to Karen Magnussen, the Canadian champion, who skated a very strong, careful performance. Janet took the loss gracefully. But she would not change her mind about retiring. "I can't go on," she said. "I've skated my last competition."

ALTHOUGH I finished in fifth place, I was chosen to go on the International Skating Union (I.S.U.) tour which follows the World Championships each year. The tour helps raise money for amateur skaters and also gives skaters an opportunity to perform before different audiences in an exhibition format. Travel and accommodations were paid for, and in addition, the Amateur Association allowed each skater to be paid a few dollars per city. The Association considered these payments expense money, but to me they meant a little financial independence.

I loved touring with the other skaters, many of whom were now my friends. Gordie McKellen was there, always the life and soul of the group. He was never without a funny remark or a practical joke. My mother, who came along as chaperon, became the butt of some of these jokes, but she took it all in stride.

Mom had brought her camera to record the trip for posterity. She photographed everything in sight and Gordie egged her on unmercifully. "Quick, Mrs. Hamill," he would say. "There's another lake coming up—get ready!" Mother would fumble with her camera, trying to advance the film quickly. "It's a one-of-a-kind lake, Mrs. Hamill," Gordie would say urgently. "Don't miss it." And so Mom traversed Europe, hanging out the windows of trains and buses, well on her way to amassing the most extensive collection of lake photographs in history.

When we traveled into East Germany we were surprised to find everything very cold and uninviting. Dresden seemed to be made entirely of gray concrete and there was nothing much to do. Gordie and I played endless pranks in order to amuse ourselves. Outside our hotel was a large stone fountain. The water was turned off at nights and came on again at seven in the morning. One night Gordie crept out in the dark and emptied a giant packet of soap flakes into the bottom of the fountain. We stayed up all night waiting to see the fountain start up in the morning. At seven the bubbles started flying everywhere and sailed across the quad into the hotel lobby. Everyone knew who had done it.

As the tour neared its end, my mother and I decided to spend a couple of days in Vienna on our way back to America. I had seen a beautiful enameled sapphire ring in a jewelry shop the year before and wondered if it would still be there. I was thrilled to find that it was. With the gift from Mrs. Fleming and the earnings from the tour, I had just enough to buy it. I have always tried to find a special piece of jewelry to remind me of each place I visit. These pieces have enormous sentimental value for me. When I wear them, they bring back memories of Sapporo, Bratislava, Calgary, St. Gervais, Toronto. And every time I look at the watch on my wrist I remember the happy times with Marcia in Oberstdorf.

THAT SUMMER–1973–I went back to Toronto to work with Ellen Burka and Brian Foley.

Brian Foley is a slightly built man who radiates energy and charisma. He doesn't just walk into a room—he explodes. Running Canada's largest dance studio, working with many top figure skaters, traversing the globe conducting master classes, and directing stage and television shows, he takes life on the run. When Brian works with a student—no matter how tired he might be at the time—he gives one hundred percent of himself. He has a genius for drawing out whatever is best in each skater and each dancer, inspiring them and releasing their creative energy. It is impossible to be inhibited around Brian. He drives his students, as he drives himself, to be total about everything they do—about life, about art, about performance. "When you're out there," he told me once, "you have to give everything away. You can't hold back—not even a little—or they will never forgive you."

Brian was certainly not inhibited. The first time he ever went to a World Championship, he was with Val and Sandra Bezic, the great Canadian champions, who were competing in the pairs event. Towards the end of their grueling five-minute free skating program, they began to lose momentum. Brian, seeing what was happening, shot up from his seat, bounded down the steps of the arena and ran around the ice barriers, stopping right in front of them. They were performing a death spiral just before their last series of footwork and jumps. Brian waited until they had come out of the spiral, then he waved his fur hat at Sandra yelling, "Come on, Sandra—*Move your ass!*"

As Sandra and Val picked up pace, he made his way back to the skaters' entrance and waited for them to finish, oblivious to all the curious stares from startled onlookers. He was going to motivate his skaters any way he could.

THAT FALL my mother and I were back in Denver in yet another gloomy apartment. The competitive cycle was underway again and I was getting up at five A.M. every weekday to be on the ice by six. Some mornings I was fortunate enough to have access to five o'clock ice—although as I struggled out of bed at four-thirty in the morning I didn't feel very fortunate. I would stand beside my bed, eyes bleary, swaying back and forth trying to persuade myself that it was all worth it.

Janet Lynn had now retired from the amateur skating world and signed a huge three-year contract to skate in the Ice Follies. I was now the number one contender for the U.S. Senior Ladies' title. I tried not to think about it because I was afraid the pressure would overwhelm me. I just went to the rink each day and tried to concentrate. Carlo seemed satisfied with my progress.

My mother was lonely. For the second year in a row, she was faced with the choice of sitting at the ice rink all day or going home to our cheerless apartment. There was no money to do anything frivolous. At home in Riverside she had belonged to many clubs and had led a busy social life, seeing friends on a regular basis. Here she had little chance to meet people. She always came with me to the early morning sessions—probably because I was often the only one there at that hour. But as soon as the other skaters began to arrive she slipped away and went home.

Together we decided that she needed a companion. We found a tiny, loveable Lhasa Apso puppy, so small he fit perfectly into my mother's hand. Our lease stated clearly that we were not allowed to keep pets, so we bought some large pillow cases. Each day we put little Chops into a pillow case, told him to be very quiet and carried him down the stairs as laundry. At night we brought him back into the apartment the same way. Our neighbors must have thought us excessively clean since we obviously did a load of laundry every single day.

AT THE END of January I won my first Ladies' Senior title in Providence, Rhode Island. I had mixed feelings about the victory. Going to the World Championships as the National gold medalist is a major political advantage and I was thrilled to be the National Champion—I had worked for that for a long time. Standing on the winner's

*1974 National
Championships.
School figures, above,
The Hamill Camel, right*

podium waving to the crowd was a thrill I shall never forget. On the other hand, I felt an ever heavier responsibility—not just to myself, my family and Carlo, but also to my country. I would be carrying America's hopes with me too. It was a little frightening.

Carlo was concerned about how I would handle the pressure. As we trained for the Worlds, he tried to prepare me mentally. "You have to skate for yourself," he told me. "In the end, when you are out there alone, you must forget all about the others. You just concentrate hard on what you are doing and skate the very best way you know how. If you lose your concentration you will fall."

U.S. World Team, 1974: from left to right—Terry Kubicka, me, Juli McKinstry, Kath Malmberg, Randy Garner, Tai Reina Babilonia, Johnny Johns, Melissa Militano, Gordon McKellen Jr., Colleen O'Connor, Jim Millns

He told my mother to make sure I got lots of rest. "A tired skater," he told her, "is a careless skater. Dorothy must have a clear head and a sharp mind."

LATE IN February we left for Munich, the site of the 1974 World Championship. Olympia Halle, which seats ten thousand people, is one of the largest and finest arenas in all of Europe. The German people have always been great skating fans, and I think of Munich as the capital city of the skating world.

I was among the favorites for the Ladies' title and although I would never have admitted it, somewhere deep down I believed I might be able to win the gold medal. Hope stirred inside me like restless butterflies.

The Men's championship was especially exciting at Munich. Toller Cranston, who had just won his fourth Canadian championship, was an important painter in Canada where he founded the School of Mystic Symbolism. He was also a ground-breaking free skater and had developed new moves, added new dimensions. He was a major influence on the sport, and yet, so far, he had never won a world medal.

Another popular competitor was John Curry, the great English skater who had just captured the European title. In his own way, John brought just as large an influence to bear on male skating as Toller. He had years of classical ballet training which he incorporated into his work on ice. He brought an exquisite pure line to his art.

In the end, neither Toller nor John won the gold medal. It went instead to the flaxen-haired East German, Jan Hoffman. Second place went to the Russian, Sergei Volkov. Toller Cranston turned in an extraordinary free skating performance to win the bronze medal, and John Curry finished fourth overall. But

Toller, clearly the favorite of the German fans, had something unique in store for them in his exhibition at the Sunday afternoon show following the competition.

Toller Cranston had long been a lover of opera, but the International Skating Union prohibits the use of vocal music in competitive performances. However, in the exhibition event following the Worlds, Toller chose to demonstrate the potential of marrying two art forms—opera and ice. He skated to the famous aria from *I Pagliacci,* and as Canio's tragic laugh rang out across the arena, Toller's black-clad shape slowly unfolded. His interpretation of the tragic story captivated us all and we watched breathlessly until the final dramatic moments of his performance. Then in one movement the entire audience stood up and applauded wildly. It was one of the great performances in skating history.

I WAS TERRIBLY nervous before the free skating. I had placed fifth in figures and moved into third after the short program. I was in the running for the gold. "Relax," Carlo kept telling me. But he was a nervous wreck himself. The Olympia Halle was packed to the rafters, and I couldn't wait to get out on the ice.

Just before me was the local German girl, Gerti Schandrel. She had placed tenth after compulsories and although she was not a particularly strong free skater, she gave a fine performance. When she finished, the hometown crowd leaped to its feet and started to cheer and stamp. I was standing at the entrance, waiting to go out. Gerti didn't come off the ice right away, so I took off my skate guards and began to warm up.

Gerti's marks were announced—5.5s and 5.4s. Excellent marks for her, but the crowd was furious—they wanted her to get sixes. They began to boo loudly. The more they booed, the more she waved and smiled at them. Finally the announcer called my name. As I started to skate forward the booing intensified. I wasn't sure what to do, so I circled around and came back to the barrier. Gerti was still on the ice blowing kisses to the crowd.

The announcer called my name again and Carlo gave me a gentle shove and sent me out to center ice. I took up my position and heard the crowd roar their objections. It was deafening.

The announcer repeated my name, trying to quiet the crowd. The boos grew louder and I was devastated. I couldn't understand why the people hated me so much. I looked over to the entrance in a panic, trying to find Carlo. I didn't know what to do. Then the tears came, pouring down my cheeks unchecked, and suddenly I couldn't stand it any longer. I turned and fled off the ice into Carlo's arms. "I can't skate," I sobbed. "They hate me." Carlo tried to calm me, but was so upset himself that he only made things worse.

Finally the referee told me to get my skate guards and wait in the dressing room until the commotion had died down. As I stepped out to pick up my guards, the announcer, thinking I was about to skate, announced me again.

"From the United States, Miss Dorothy Hamill."

The audience broke into enthusiastic cheers—I believe they were trying to reassure me that their display of antagonism had not been meant for me, but for the judges. I looked back at my dad and shrugged. So long as they were cheering I might as well go out and skate.

I skated one of my best performances and thought I might have taken the gold medal. But in the end first place went to the tiny pixie-like East German skater, Christine Errath. She had turned in an outstanding performance and held onto her lead. I placed second, and Dianne de Leeuw, from Holland, placed third.

Back in the hotel I struggled with an overpowering flood of emotion. I was crushed, disappointed, let down. I had anticipated victory but was tasting defeat. In the end it was my dad who helped me come to grips with it.

"You did the best you could," he said quietly. "That's all you can ever ask of yourself."

And so I accepted it. The butterflies of hope folded their wings and waited. There was always next year.

Congratulating East Germany's Christine Errath, 1974 Worlds

1975 Worlds, Colorado Springs

FOURTEEN

The Face of Failure

*T*HAT spring I went on tour with the I.S.U. group again. When we returned home I wanted a rest. Carlo wanted me to go right back to training for the 1975 championships, which were to be in Colorado Springs, on home territory. But it was far too early for me to even begin to think about them. I just went about my life and let the summer slip past. I visited my grandparents in Rockport and savored the peace and the silence. I tried to memorize the sound of the water and the smell of the pines so that they would stay with me during the long, winter months.

In late summer I went back to Toronto to get my new programs choreographed by Mrs. Burka and Brian Foley. Then it was back to Denver and Carlo's demanding schedule. In one way things were looking up: I was beginning to anticipate the next World Championship; I was actually looking forward to it. But in other ways the pressure was beginning to build again. Now that I was National Champion, the eyes of the U.S.F.S.A. were on me. We were less than two years from the 1976 Innsbruck Olympics and winning the World title in 1975 would greatly increase my chances of becoming the Olympic champion.

My family was feeling the strain of my competitive career

too. Back in Connecticut my dad was alone most of the time—Marcia was now in college studying microbiology. Sandy was at Yale studying medicine. It was a lonely life for Dad. Mother was in Denver with me. She tried to be cheerful, driving me back and forth to the rink, trying to think of things we could do that didn't involve ice. But I knew she missed her life back home. She had been a nursery school teacher and was used to playing bridge and bowling regularly. I did my best to keep her company, and Chops helped a lot.

I had no idea then how severe our financial crisis had become. The cost of skating had reached astronomical proportions. It was the extraordinary things that made it so expensive. I used custom boots, so skates alone ran about six hundred dollars a year. Costumes were from one to three hundred dollars each, depending on whether my mom made them herself or not. On top of all this came the trips to Toronto for new choreography, training periods in Lake Placid and Colorado, music tapes, membership fees in clubs and in the U.S.F.S.A. Most expensive of all were the actual competitions: air fares for myself and my coach, hotel expenses, payment for my coach's time. The list seemed endless. But these costs were not peculiar to my career—they were the constant nightmare faced by every top competitive skater.

My school life was going smoothly. I was enrolled in the Colorado Academy, a very good private school. I had a lot of friends there but saw little of them outside of classes. Instead I hung out with the kids from the rink—going to parties and occasionally giving one myself. What fun we had at those parties, laughing and throwing pillows and practicing our jumps like maniacs on one another's beds. We broke the springs on my bed one night trying to do a double axel. We never had any money—any of us—but it didn't seem to matter much. We had enough for hot chocolate and potato chips and sometimes we went to the drive-in movies. At least one of us did. He would drive up to the ticket barrier, buy a ticket, drive into the movie, park a long way from the entrance and get out of the car. Then he would open the trunk to let the rest of us out.

IN NOVEMBER I was invited to perform in Superskates, a huge benefit exhibition held in Madison Square Garden to raise money for the Olympic team. I was very excited about it. I trained hard, practicing a new show number I had learned in Toronto during the summer.

Through friends of my parents I had met a boy named Chris who was a Harvard student. He had written asking me to go to the Harvard-Yale football game with him. Mom liked Chris and encouraged me to go. The game was two days before Superskates so it seemed to work out perfectly. I would fly to Boston, go to the game, stay with my grandparents and then go home to Connecticut where Dad would take me to Superskates.

On Friday, the morning of my flight to Boston, I went to the rink to run through my program one last time. John Curry was there and he gave me some helpful suggestions. I had done dozens of double axels that day, but I wanted to be absolutely sure they were right. I decided to do just one more. As I prepared to take off, my foot got stuck in a rut in the ice, and my body kept turning from the momentum. I felt a searing pain shoot through my leg as I fell to the ice.

John skated over to me. "Get up Dorothy, and skate around," he said. "Just once, no matter how much it hurts. You mustn't lose your nerve."

I tried hard to stand and almost blacked out from the pain. "Come on," John insisted. "Just once. Trust me." And so I did—I still don't know how I made it around, but as soon as I reached the exit I came off the ice and tried to take my boots off.

My foot was already so swollen I had to unlace that boot right to the bottom before I could get it off. "It'll be okay," I assured everyone. "It'll be just fine." I was so anxious to see Chris and take my trip that I wasn't going to admit that anything was wrong.

By the time I got home I realized that it was my knee that hurt the most. I ran it under ice cold water to see if that would help. When my mother came in I hid the pain from her. I could hardly put any weight on the leg at all, but she didn't notice. I made the plane to Boston and all the way there I kept my foot up, trying to ease the throbbing. I knew by now that I was really hurt.

When I arrived in Boston, I looked around the airport for Chris, but he wasn't there. I sat miserably on a bench trying to take my mind off the pain in my leg. Finally, an hour later, he arrived. He made no excuses and seemed to have no sympathy for my pain. He insisted I walk to the car.

We went straight to a party where I sat with my foot propped up on a chair while he moved around the room chatting with everyone. I was still pretending to myself that everything would be all right in the end. When he finally dropped me off at my grandparents' house it was midnight.

My father had called at eleven and left a message for me to call back. He had been furious to find I was still out and even angrier that I hadn't called Bill. Jonsie was in the hospital, and Bill had been deeply worried when I was late. I felt terrible and crawled away to bed to spend a restless night trying to find a comfortable position for my leg.

The next morning the pain seemed a little easier and Bill

took me to visit Jonsie in the hospital. She looked so frail lying there, but her wits were about her.

"What's the matter, child?" she demanded. "What've you done to your foot?"

I was amazed—Jonsie always knew me better than anyone. I found myself confessing to her, and she called one of the doctors and asked him to take a look at me. "This is my granddaughter," she told him sternly. "She is a skating champion and you'd better take good care of her."

He examined my knee and my ankle and patted me on the arm. "Just a bit of a twist," he assured me. "Nothing to worry about. It'll heal by itself in no time." The ankle was puffed up like a balloon, but I wanted to believe he was right.

Chris picked me up and took me to the game, but by the time we had parked the car and walked across the rough gravel of the parking lot to the stadium, the pain had become almost unbearable. I couldn't find a comfortable way to sit, and I couldn't have been very good company. Chris became more and more irritated with me. Harvard won the game and he was assuming that I would stay for the celebrations, but I had already planned to be home in Connecticut that night.

It was a three-hour drive, and by the time we arrived I knew our brief romance was over. My father was far from pleased with him and he made no bones about it. Chris soon said goodbye, got into his car and drove away, out of my life. I never saw him again.

When Dad saw my ankle he was furious. "Why on earth didn't you tell anyone?" he asked. I told him I had been afraid I wouldn't be allowed to go to the game. I also repeated what the doctor had told me in Jonsie's hospital. "He must have been blind," Dad said angrily. "This leg is in terrible shape."

The next morning—Sunday—Dad took me to the hospital in Connecticut for x-rays. They showed nothing. Then we drove into New York for the rehearsals in Madison Square Garden. I tried to get my foot into my boot and couldn't. The pain was just too much. We talked to the officials, and they arranged for me to see a doctor in New Jersey. I also saw a specialist in New York. No one could find anything wrong. No tendons pulled, no bones broken, nothing. So they told me I had to skate. I was hysterical. All Monday morning I tried to rehearse and cried most of the time from the pain.

In the middle of this rehearsal period I had a run-in with the press. Reporters had always been kind and helpful before this, but now a photographer was trying to take pictures of me and I was fighting back tears and trying to look normal for him. "Can't you do any better than that?" he asked. "You look like you just lost your wallet."

Tenley Albright came in after lunch. She had been an Olympic and World Champion in the 1950s, then had become a surgeon. She took a look at my ankle and suggested I tape it up and try to skate on it. But it was no good. I sat there in tears wondering what I could do.

Finally Dad told the officials he was not going to let me skate. A doctor, whose little girl was also a skater, had come over and warned us that I could worsen the injury even by walking on the leg. "Olympics are only a year away," he told Dad. "Nothing is worth risking that."

But the officials were adamant. I was the National Champion; I was expected to skate. They wouldn't hear of me pulling out. So I taped up my ankle, taped up my knee, swallowed a lot of strong pills a doctor had given me, and went onto the ice. I did only one number and didn't jump at all, but when I had finished the pain was making colored lights explode inside my head. That was my first taste of political pressure. I realized suddenly that as long as I wanted to stay within the system, I was at the mercy of the Amateur Association.

Back in Colorado an orthopedic doctor recommended immobilizing the ankle for a couple of months to see if it improved. He made a walking cast for me. I could hobble around just fine—but I couldn't skate. It was already November, and the National Championships in Oakland were less than twelve weeks away.

At the end of the month Mom went home. Jonsie was still very weak after her stay in the hospital and needed careful nursing. Mom worried about leaving me alone, but in a funny way, it was a welcome relief. Living cramped together in a small room added to the frustration of my not being able to skate, had made us irritable. Besides, I was seventeen and I wanted some privacy. We fought constantly and often ended up not speaking. I felt stifled.

I had become friends with a boy in my class at school, Bill Peavy. He had a great sense of humor and we got along very well together. I liked his family too. When Mom left, they invited me to spend Christmas with them and I accepted eagerly. They made me feel very welcome and I was happier than I had been in a long time.

I was scheduled to get my cast off right after Christmas. With the Nationals so close I would have to go back on the ice immediately if I was to have any chance of getting back into competitive shape. I tried hard to keep fit in the meantime with lots of stretching exercises and waist bends. On December 26th the doctor took my cast off and two hours later I had my skates on. Stroking around the rink again after so long felt wonderful.

A FEW WEEKS later I was in Oakland for the Nationals. I was a nervous wreck. This was the one chance for the year, and if I failed to place, I wouldn't even be going to the Worlds in Colorado Springs. Somehow I pulled it off, winning the gold for the second time. I was very shaky in my long program, but at least I didn't fall, and I even managed to land a double axel. The next day, however, the ankle was back to square one. The pain was terrible. I tried taping it but it didn't help and I was in despair. I was imagining plaster casts again and was convinced that I would never be able to skate in the Worlds that year.

Then someone told us about a sports physiotherapist in Denver who had worked with many hockey players. He gave me ultrasound treatments—it seemed that he was only rubbing a cold metal thing on my leg, but apparently it worked. After two weeks the pain had disappeared. It seemed like a miracle.

I began to work furiously for the Colorado Springs Worlds—after all, I would be the hometown girl this year. Carlo made me concentrate on my double axel, which was a required element for the short compulsory program. Because the short program counted for twenty percent of the overall marks, it was very important to complete all of its seven required elements correctly.

By the sixth of March the Broadmoor Hotel in Colorado Springs was swarming with the elite of the skating world. John Curry and Toller Cranston were again favored for the Men's titles. Dianne de Leeuw, Christine Errath and I were considered to be the favorites for the Ladies' title and the great Russian pair skaters Rodnina and Zaitsev were once again the clear favorites for their event. The legendary Russian ice dance team of Pakhimova and Gorshkov were sidelined because of Gorshkov's pneumonia. It was anybody's medal in ice dance, and Colleen O'Connor and Jim Millns, the United States ice dance champions, were the hometown hopefuls.

Again the Men's title eluded both John and Toller. Sergei Volkov and Vladimir Kovalev took the gold and the silver medals for Russia. John Curry skated superbly in the free skating to win the bronze medal, and Toller placed a close fourth. Rodnina and Zaitsev took the Pairs Championship easily. Rodnina seemed incapable of making a mistake as she jumped and spun her way around the rink. In the ice dance Colleen O'Connor and Jim

With Carlo Fassi, 1975 Worlds

Free skating, Worlds, 1975

Millns looked to be in a good position to take the gold medal. They skated an outstanding free dance; the crowd cheered wildly as they executed fast and intricate footwork without a flaw. But in the end they lost to two young Russian dancers—Minenkov and Moiseeva, later to become affectionately known as "Minnie and Moe."

The Ladies' final was on Saturday evening—the last phase of the entire competition. I was not particularly well placed after school figures, but felt I could pull up in my short program. I was fairly sure I could land my double axel. I was having no pain in my ankle so wasn't worried about the leg giving out. When I landed the double axel easily, I began to enjoy the rest of my program—I had done all the difficult things. And then, right before the end, I fell on my flying sit spin. I still don't know how it happened. I don't think I have ever fallen on one before or since, but I did it that day. After that I had no chance to win the championship. Dianne de Leeuw had skated solid figures and a good short program. I skated well in the long program but not well enough to beat Dianne. She was the new World Champion and I was second again. This time Christine Errath finished third.

I was devastated. I could have forgiven myself if I'd fallen on a double axel, but to go down on a flying sit spin was intolerable. I felt I had thrown away a whole year's work because of a split second of carelessness. Worse, I felt I had let Carlo down.

I came to realize that spring that by missing the World Championship twice in a row, I had built up all the pressure for 1976. In the space of only a few months I would compete in the Nationals as defending champion, in the Olympics as a representative of the United States, and then—perhaps—in the Worlds, which I still had not won. By that time I would be nearly twenty years old, and would have skated competitions for ten years.

Layback spin, Olympics, 1976

FIFTEEN

The Rainbow's End

$\mathcal{F}$OLLOWING the Worlds we toured North America for the I.S.U. The great thing about the I.S.U. tour was that you could skate just for the fun of it and relax after the pressure of the Worlds. As we set out from Colorado Springs I tried hard to forget the disappointment of what I considered to be the worst failure of my life. It took a few days, but by the time we reached California I was beginning to mend and was once again able to join in the fun.

When we were in San Diego we drove across the border to Tijuana and purchased, among other things, some small and harmless bombs that could be inserted into the cigarettes of unsuspecting victims. Since my mother was one of the few people who smoked on that tour, she was selected as the first victim. I assured everyone that she wouldn't mind in the least. Poor Mom—it blew up beautifully, right on time and singed one of her eyebrows, but she was a very good sport about it and managed to laugh after she had recovered from the shock. "For a moment," she said, "I thought Gordie was back." Unfortunately he wasn't. He had retired the year before and was teaching in Lake Placid.

During the tour I heard about a show in Cleveland, Ohio.

The show was to be produced later in the spring by Charles A. DeMore, the president of the United States Figure Skating Association, and a large newspaper advertisement had announced that I would be the star. I knew nothing about it. Mom telephoned Cleveland to find out what was going on. They confirmed that the programs were already printed and included me as the star performer.

My mother got mad. "You'll just have to change it," she told them. "Dorothy hasn't been asked to skate a Cleveland show. She knows nothing about it. And in any case she couldn't possibly miss any more school."

I had missed two whole months of school, February and March, and was taking correspondence courses in order to keep up. My school in Denver was very helpful and was trying to ensure that I could graduate that summer along with everyone else. But to miss any more school now would be out of the question. It could set me back a year and saddle me with school during the last vital year of training for the Olympics.

When we returned to Denver we received an official invitation from Chuck DeMore to skate the Cleveland show. Mom telephoned him and explained why I couldn't come. He told her it would only be for a week.

"No," Mom said firmly. "It would also entail the training and the traveling. She can't do it; she has to finish school."

Mr. DeMore took another tack; he suggested that I wouldn't want to let the Amateur Association down.

Mom still refused to say yes. I was going to finish school, she said, graduate on time and attend my senior prom. And that, as far as she was concerned, was that.

Then the show organizers called and pleaded with my mother. They had sold tickets by advertising my participation, and people would be angry if I didn't come. Mom had the school guidance counselor call them back to explain the academic situation. But still they kept it up.

I was torn. As the United States Champion I had a position to uphold. I was an ambassador for skating. I was expected to be able to carry out that function. I had a responsibility—an *obligation*—to my country and to my Association to skate this show. If I refused, I was afraid they would assume that I did not take my duties as Champion seriously.

Terrified of the possible political consequences of refusing further, I finally agreed. I missed more school and was not able to graduate with my friends. Then I spent the whole summer in school catching up and managed to pass my final exams. I graduated but I never did make the Senior Prom.

IN SEPTEMBER I began my final training pattern for the Olympics. Without school to worry about it was in some ways easier than earlier years. But in other ways it was more difficult. I skated longer hours—seven, eight hours a day. I would start at five and work on figures for four hours or more. Then after lunch I would free skate for several hours. I was under a great deal of pressure now. I could feel the tension. There were days when I simply couldn't get anything right and became so frustrated that I would yell and kick the ice and rage at myself for being so stupid. How could I have done it so perfectly yesterday and now couldn't do it at all? How was that possible? The younger kids would look at me and figure I was mad at them for getting in my way. I was just mad at myself. My mom would be furious when she saw me pull one of these tantrums. She would take me aside and tell me there were cheaper ways of wasting time than this and that if I was going to skate I should get out there and do it. I would go back to the ice and start over and try to get everything right.

It was getting harder and harder to get up in the morning. I was the only one left from the original crowd at the rink. Most of the others had quit. John Curry trained with Carlo, but he didn't come in as early as I did. He arrived at ten o'clock and did two or three hours of figures, free skated a bit and went home. In the evening session he came back and free skated again. I really think he had it right. But I kept up those early morning figure sessions. I was like a zombie so it's difficult to imagine that I really accomplished very much. But then again— maybe I did.

It was good to have John around to watch. I learned a lot from studying him free skate, and he was always ready to help me with my own style. John is a purist. He doesn't downplay

With Carlo Fassi, working on school figures

technique as so many try to do. He embodies it, taking the most basic movements and turning them into an art form with superb lines and edges. Some time after the Olympics John skated a number created for him by the famous dance choreographer, Twyla Tharp. It was called "After All" and I still think of it with pleasure. It was a starkly elegant ballet which incorporated school figures—those dreaded circles and twists—and made them into something immensely beautiful and memorable. I think perhaps John's most important contribution is that he has brought such credibility to skating in its own right, giving it dignity and raising it to a level of fine art.

In late September I went to Toronto to work with Ellen Burka and Brian Foley. My Olympic long program was already set, but it still needed a lot of work. Mrs. Burka started re-choreographing it. She found a new piece of music for the slow section and also set my short program, carefully matching each of the required elements to the music. Day after day we would work on the programs, going over every detail carefully. "Don't forget the fingers," she would say. "The hands. The arms. Feel the music in every part of you. Let it flow out of your fingers." I felt the tension leaving me and began to skate better.

Brian Foley came with Mrs Burka for the late night sessions and stood with his head tilted to one side, feet tapping and cigar clamped between his fingers. At the end he would motion me over to him, suggest some changes and then run down the ice beside me as I went through the program again.

"Up—*Up!*" he would yell. "Hold it—*Hold it!*"

I would finish my final scratch spin and look to him for approval.

"Good girl," he'd say. "Much better. Now let's do it again and this time I want you to *move your ass.*"

What inspiration those two were—how they could lift spirits

With Brian Foley

and strengthen resolve. I wished with all my heart that they lived in Colorado.

I did Superskates in Madison Square Garden that November. Later I skated for the Jimmy Fund in Boston, an exhibition to raise funds for the Harvard Cancer Center. The Jimmy Fund Show had been started by John Misha Petkevich, so I was especially pleased to be able to skate in it. John Misha had retired from skating and was now a Rhodes Scholar at Oxford. After the Jimmy Fund Show I went back to Colorado and settled in for the last stretch of training before competitions. I made up my mind that I would block out everything—I would concentrate totally. I was going for the gold.

TOWARDS THE END of November a family crisis changed my routine. My grandfather Bill had taken a bad fall and was very frail. Jonsie, who had been in and out of the hospital herself, could not cope with him on her own. They needed to be with their family. Mom didn't want to leave me on my own during the Olympic year, yet she felt that she couldn't leave Bill and Jonsie alone either. Our problem was solved when TeriAnn and Brent Landis, two of my friends from school, invited me to stay with them.

Dr. and Mrs. Landis treated me like one of their own and I immediately felt at home. I also felt some of the pressure lift. They knew nothing about skating and it was a relief to be able to go home from the rink and hear normal conversation and watch television or play cards. No one ever asked me if I had landed my double axel that day.

Diet had become very important. Skating so early in the morning, I couldn't eat a heavy breakfast; yet if I didn't eat anything I soon became nauseous. Eventually I discovered a wonderful hot cereal which gave me energy and satisfied my hunger without being heavy. I also took vitamin pills—vitamin C to counteract the effects of the cold (or so I liked to think)— and iron capsules, and I made my sandwiches out of whole wheat bread. I was determined not to come down with the flu before the Olympics.

Part of my health plan included working out with a physical trainer six days a week. I went to his gym in the afternoons right after free skating to work out with weights, run on a treadmill and ride a bicycle with increasingly heavy weights attached to my feet. I watched my muscles getting bigger and bigger. My legs seemed like tree trunks. He made me eat wheat germ and drink a whole bottle of awful mineral water a day— stuff so horrible that I gagged on it. The bigger my muscles got the lower my jumps became. My skating was deteriorating rapidly. I was convinced it was the result of these physical training methods.

I went home for Christmas and afterwards my mom came back with me. She had made arrangements for someone to be with my grandparents so she could look after me in the final weeks before the Olympics. She was horrified at what had happened to my skating. I told her I wanted to stop going to the trainer. I couldn't take it. So two weeks before the Nationals, I gave it up. Within two days everyone could see the difference in me. My legs grew smaller, and my jumps grew bigger. My confidence increased and I no longer dragged myself from one day to the next waiting only for sleep.

We did have to worry about other nagging physical problems. The year before, I had run into minor trouble with my back, so I had to be careful to warm up thoroughly or the pain would return. The long training sessions before the Olympics were also very hard on my neck and shoulders. A lot of skaters suffer from tension in those areas. Twice a week, on Mondays and Fridays, I went to a health club and sat in the whirlpool and the sauna. How I looked forward to those visits. After the sauna I had a Japanese massage on my neck. I could feel the big knot dissolving. On days when I couldn't go to the health club I used to sit in a hot tub for hours at night, soaking. Only part of my feeling of exhaustion was physical; the rest was from the emotional pressure.

THE National Championships were in Colorado Springs at the end of January, earlier than usual because of the Olympics. Even though I won the Ladies' title again, I was far from pleased with my performance.

I felt I was falling apart. One of the problems was Carlo. I sensed that he was losing interest in me. Perhaps he felt he had done all he could. I don't know. But for whatever reason, it seemed to me that he was paying me very little attention. He spent very little time training me. I felt rejected. I walked around carrying this inside of me, feeling very miserable. And yet to the outside world I was the Golden Girl. No one had any idea anything was wrong.

After the Nationals Carlo left to supervise John Curry at the European Championship. I was alone and I began to panic. Not knowing what else to do, my mother asked Peter Burrows to help me out. Peter teaches in the New York area and I knew him from my days at the Skyrink. Although he was not my coach, there was never a day when he hadn't asked me how I was feeling and if there was anything he could do to help. Peter agreed in an instant to assist me in making final preparations for the Olympics. So we came back to New York and I trained at the Skyrink again. Peter pulled my head together, helped me to focus, inspired me and motivated me. Suddenly I was back in one piece again and skating as well as I'd ever skated. I felt a surge of hope. I could still do it.

SINCE MY disastrous haircut in London in 1972, I had been searching for a good stylist who could manage my very difficult hair. Melissa Militano, who had

With Peter Burrows

always been my idea of a fashion-setter in the skating world, had her hair cut by a Japanese stylist named Suga in New York. He had found the secret of styling a skater's hair so that it would fall back into place easily. The only problem was that he was booked up for months ahead. My dad pleaded with him. "Please," he said, "my daughter is going to the Olympics. She desperately needs a haircut." Suga finally took pity on us and at seven o'clock one evening, with his scissors in one hand and his brush in the other, he surveyed my face, my head, my hair and then my entire body. He told me he never cut two people's hair the same. He tailored the hair to suit the entire person in every way. So he stood there and he thought and then he started to cut. After a while he stopped and disappeared into the other room to watch something on television. I sat there wondering if he was finished. I wasn't sure if I was supposed to stay or not. But after a while he came out again, wet the hair down and started to cut again. When he finished I couldn't believe it. For the first time I could remember my hair looked good. I didn't have to go out on the streets and cry about it.

Just before I left for the Olympics *Time* magazine took some photographs of me. They shot hundreds of them. ABC–TV also asked me to skate for the "Up Close and Personal" segment they were doing for their Olympic coverage. I remember doing hundreds of layback spins, one after the other, while the cameras shot me from overhead towers. I didn't really think too much about any of this at the time. Thanks to Peter Burrows, my mind was entirely on my skating.

Peter had been so helpful that my mother asked the U.S.F.S.A. if he could go with us to Innsbruck as my coach. But the Association refused: Carlo Fassi was my coach on record and he was to be there. Mom was furious. She tried everything to get them to change their minds, but it was no use. Finally she took

*U.S. Team, 1976 Olympics: from left to right, first row—Terry Kubicka,
Randy Gardner, Bill Fauver, Andy Stroukoff. Second row—Suzie Kelly, Wendy
Burge, me, Judy Genovese, Alice Cook, Colleen O'Connor, Linda Fratianni, Tai
Babilonia. Third row—U.S.F.S.A. Team Leader Dr. Franklin Nelson, David
Santee, Kent Weigle, Jim Millns, Dr. Hugh C. Graham*

comfort in the knowledge that Ellen Burka and Brian Foley were
both planning to be there.

INNSBRUCK WAS alive with spec-
ulation. Once again my main rivals were Dianne de Leeuw and
Christine Errath. Dianne was now the reigning World Champion and probably had the inside edge. Carlo warned me not to
think about it, to put it out of my mind. He said he was pleased
with the shape I was in, and we were working well together. I
felt good.

The mood in the Olympic Village was strange. Now that I was a veteran of international competition, I knew many of the other skaters. But we all went around as if we were in cocoons, not communicating with each other. People seemed to be afraid that if they spoke—if they let anyone else in on what they were thinking—they might somehow take away from their chances for a medal. The path to the Olympic Games is a long and a hard one, and when you are there you simply don't do anything that might compromise you.

We had very little ice time—a maximum of two hours a day—and there was little to do to fill up the hours between practice sessions, so I gave interviews to radio stations, television stations and newspapers. I was happy to do it but I had no clear idea that I was the focus of an enormous media explosion back home in the States.

In the Olympic Village we were pretty well insulated. One day, however, I was handed a copy of the International edition of *Time* magazine. I was on the cover. We had always had a subscription to *Time* and I had read cover stories about politicians and film stars, kings and space explorers. It was difficult to comprehend that I was now reading about myself.

Carlo said he was very pleased with the shape I was in. My mom's hopes of Ellen Burka and Brian Foley being there to help me through the final days were not fulfilled. Mrs. Burka was there but her total attention was centered around Toller Cranston, who was making his last attempt to win a gold medal. Brian Foley never got to Innsbruck. On the morning he was to leave Toronto, he received a telegram from the Canadian team requesting that he stay away from the Games. It did not explain further. Deeply hurt, Brian took his family to Hawaii for the week. As a result of what he interpreted to be a political move, Brian severed his connection with amateur skating. It was a sad blow to all the young competitors who might have gained from his energy and his love.

I had heard about athletes trying to psyche each other out during important competitions, and I got my first experience of this during the Olympics. One night when Carlo and I were walking back from practice we noticed a car coming right toward us. I recognized the occupants as another skater and her coach. I lifted my hand to wave to them when suddenly Carlo grabbed my arm and pulled me roughly onto the grass at the side of the road. Just then the car accelerated, running right over the spot I had been standing on a moment before. I was shaken, but the driver of the car just laughed and drove away.

JOHN CURRY was skating brilliantly in practice sessions. I watched him run through his Olympic program and felt very fortunate to have been able to train with him for the past year. I think I almost wanted John to win a gold medal more than I wanted it for myself. He had worked so hard and as someone who admittedly hated to compete, he had taken a courageous step in turning himself over to the system so completely. A year earlier he had almost quit skating altogether, feeling frustrated that his unique and beautiful style was not fully accepted by the World judges. But in the summer of 1975 he made up his mind that if he was ever going to be able to influence the future of skating—to express himself in the way he wished—he would first have to prove himself in the traditional skating world. He felt that he must win a World title if he was ever to be taken seriously. "I look on the Olympic medal as my skating diploma" he said. "I am determined to graduate." And he had gone to Carlo, the master teacher—the most accepted of all coaches. And although John's free skating was—and always will be—one thousand percent his own, Carlo definitely helped him in other ways. He worked miracles on John's figures—just as he had done on mine—and changed his attitude towards competition. Carlo taught him, as he taught us all, how to get it all together at the right moment.

Valuable as Carlo was to so many of us, however, the education of a figure skater is a complicated thing, dependant on many teachers. I know about free skating from Gus Lussi. Even now, when I have trouble with a jump or a spin, I go back to what Gus told me. I can still hear him saying, "Guts, Dorothy. Give it lots of guts." He would demand so much from us and we gave it. Gus taught all the great skaters—Ronnie Roberson, Dick Button, Toller Cranston, John Curry, Gordie McKellen, Hayes Jenkins. He was the one who thought up the move that came to be known as The Hamill Camel, which is a spin combination I skated in the Olympics—a flying camel layover into a sit spin. Choreography is another specialty. The routines I used for international competition were one hundred percent Ellen Burka and Brian Foley.

But the special genius of Carlo was that he could put the whole package together. He knew when to let go of a skater and when to put his foot down, and he was one of the few coaches (Mr. Lussi was another) who could be totally objective in his relationships with his students. It didn't matter to Carlo who added to a skater's repertoire or technique (provided it was a positive addition), nor did he seem threatened by any outside influence on his students. He only wanted to produce the best looking students he could. He did not, as many coaches did, live vicariously through his students, and from that point of view working with Carlo was a very healthy experience.

THE DAY of the Olympic school figures I was calmer than I had expected to be. I managed to place second, and Carlo said that put me into a very good position. The short program was next, and I skated a strong program to pull up to first. Christine Errath, Dianne de Leeuw and I were all in line for the gold medal.

The morning after the short program, my mom decided it was very important to take my mind off the long program of the next day. I was going into the free skating as the clear favorite and Mom didn't want to give me a chance to feel that pressure. She planned a day trip to Salzburg to visit the site of the *Sound of Music*. It was exactly what I needed. Mom drove Marcia, Sandy, and his wife, Perky, down in a Volkswagen bus early in the morning, and Dad and I stayed behind for the practice session. Right after it was finished we caught a train to Salzburg. When we arrived Mom had already lined up a guide who knew every nook and cranny of the city and could tell us every detail of the making of the Von Trapp movie. Marcia, Perky, and I were entranced by it all. I completely forgot about the free skating, and that night I slept soundly.

FRIDAY—the day of the Ladies' final—Mom gave me her rings. It was a tradition we had started that I would wear all her rings when I competed. I thought they would bring me luck and I wouldn't skate without them. This year I had a special ring that had led to some confusion. It had been a gift from a fan, but somehow the press got the idea that it was an engagement ring and since I had been dating the Russian skater, Vladimir Kovalev, the newspapers announced on the morning of the free skating final that I was engaged to marry him. Vladimir was as surprised by the news as I was.

Telegrams addressed to me had been pouring into the village ever since my strong finish in the figures. Before the final competition I opened them, expecting to read a name I recog-

Going for the Gold, Innsbruck

The thrill of victory!

nized, but gradually I realized these were all from complete strangers who had taken the time to wish me luck. I was overwhelmed by it. Suddenly I was carrying more than my own personal hopes and fears. I felt that in a sense I was no longer Dorothy Hamill—I was the United States. The medal was not mine to lose—I was representing the hopes and dreams of thousands of people I had never even met.

Finally—and that's the way it seemed to me then, final—I was standing out at center ice, taking deep breaths and trying to still the thudding of my heart. My knees were trembling slightly. I felt enormous pressure on me as I waited what seemed like hours for my music to start. I tried to block everything out except the skating. I tried to focus my mind, make it concentrate totally on the coming program. I remembered Mrs. Burka's words. *Make the music be the walls. Climb inside and shut everything else out.* I remembered Gus Lussi's words. *Give it everything you've got, don't hold back even the slightest bit. Attack it like a tiger.* I thought of Carlo. *Concentrate, focus, make your mind into a tunnel and look to the other end where the light is showing.* I thought of gentle Barbara and Sonya and of my parents who had helped me without complaint through all these years of preparation; and of Jonsie and Bill, who loved me no matter what I did. And then I heard the music at last and I could hear Brian Foley's words. He wasn't there, but I knew what he would have said to me. *Move your ass, Dorothy. Move your ass!*

And then I was skating and I had never felt as good as I did at that moment. I felt I possessed endless strength and I knew instinctively that I was not going to fall. I was skating better than I had ever skated in my life. Finally it had all come together, and when I had finished, I was the Olympic gold medalist. I had reached the other side of the rainbow.

The Gold!

Ice Capades

SIXTEEN

The Other Side of the Rainbow

As I stood on the winner's podium at the 1976 World Championship in Göteborg, Sweden, I knew my amateur career was over. I had achieved everything a skater could hope for. I was a National, World and Olympic Champion. I had earned the recognition of the public and the respect of my peers. The long hard years of training were finished and I was ready to move on.

My Olympic victory had brought an avalanche of inquiries from potential managers and agents, promoters and producers, all offering me get-rich-quick schemes. My dad had gone back to Connecticut right after Innsbruck, to deal with the confusion there. When I arrived home four weeks later, I found everything sorted out, waiting for me to make some decisions. I knew the most important one would be the choice of a manager—the person who would be responsible for guiding me through the maze of offers and opportunities now laid out in front of me. I spent weeks trying to make up my mind. I was wined and dined; driven in stretched limousines; bombarded with flowers and compliments. My world had changed drastically—I felt as though I were in the middle of a dream. Nothing seemed quite real.

With John Curry, I.S.U. tour following the Worlds, 1976

Finally I decided on Jerry Weintraub, an energetic, young manager from California. Jerry represented several top entertainers, including John Denver and Neil Diamond, but that had nothing to do with my choosing him. I chose him because, out of all the people I met, he was the only one who bothered to come and see me skate.

I spent a great deal of time with Jerry, trying to decide on a direction for my career. He wanted me to freelance, skating ice concerts in stadiums all over the world. He didn't want me to sign with an ice show. It would mean being tied up for forty-four weeks out of each year, and he felt that would severely limit the amount of outside work I would be able to do. But I stood my ground. I was determined to skate in one of the big shows. In the end Jerry agreed and I signed with the Ice Capades.

My three years skating full-time with the Ice Capades were very happy ones. Dick Palmer and George Eby, who are in charge of the productions, have made the Capades a special and unique environment for all the skaters. Being in the show is like being part of a large, close-knit family. I had a great deal of adjusting to do, of course. My daily routine had been turned inside out. Instead of getting up at five and going to bed early, I was now getting to bed at one or two in the morning and trying to sleep till noon. It's hard to believe now, but it took me two full years before I stopped waking up early. My eyes would open automatically at dawn.

The pressures of training had been replaced with a different kind of pressure. Now I couldn't go out without dressing up. I had to be careful of everything I said. I was required for endless publicity calls, press conferences and photographic sessions. I lived out of a trunk and seldom saw my family. Home was my hotel room, and my days off were spent on a plane traveling to the next city on the tour. But I loved it all passionately—the noise and the glitter, the costumes, the music and the lights. For me, the ice show was filled with glamour and magic.

In spite of the hectic touring schedule in those first three years with the Ice Capades, I starred in several television specials. Television was a new medium for me and I was scared to death. My first show was with Gene Kelly, who had been a favorite of mine ever since I saw him in *Singin' in the Rain.* I couldn't believe that I was actually working with him. He was kind and helpful and patient with me, and by the time we had finished the taping, I had gotten over my nervousness and was having fun. The producers, Dwight Hemion and Gary Smith, are extraordinarily talented and we have gone on to make several other shows together, with wonderful stars like Andy Williams,

With Doug Wilson, right, and Chuck Mangione, ABC's Wide World of Sports coverage, 1980 Olympics, Lake Placid

Bruce Jenner, the Osmonds, Hal Linden, Perry Como, the Carpenters and Edward Villela.

Skating for an ice show has given me real appreciation for the power and role of an audience. A responsive audience can give energy to a performer. I love to hear the audience, see their faces and know that I am communicating with them. After all, that's what the entertainment business is all about. I feel that if I can make people happy, I've done a good job, and I am always so touched when children take the time to write me letters or wait for hours in the cold to ask for my autograph.

I have often heard performers describe autograph signing as a chore, but I feel it is a compliment to be asked for an autograph. When I was twelve years old I was taken to the theater one night, and during the intermission I spotted a famous movie actor standing in the lobby. Being an autograph hound, I had brought my precious book with me, and I managed to summon up the courage to go over and ask the actor for his signature. His response was to look at me coldly, shake his head and turn back to his companion. I have never forgotten the humiliation I experienced and I vowed that—should I ever become famous— I would never unreasonably refuse to give an autograph. I have signed my name thousands of times since turning professional, and I hope I have never broken my promise.

THE FACE of professional skat-ing has changed in exciting ways since I first signed with the Ice Capades. New doors are opening and many more freelance opportunities exist than ever before. Three years ago I decided to make some changes in my career—I wanted to continue to skate in Capades, but on a more limited basis. I would perform in certain cities each year as a guest star. I also felt it was time for me to look for a new manager. My time with Jerry, though fruitful and happy, had reached an impasse. I was restless. Through my work with the Ice Capades I met Michael Rosenberg who, besides being their marketing consultant, managed the careers of several performers and sports stars. I liked Michael—he understood me and was one of the few people I had ever met who said exactly what he thought. We had often joked about his representing me, and one day I decided to ask him outright—he agreed, and we have worked together ever since.

I have finally fulfilled my long-held ambition to skate in an ice ballet. I did *The Nutcracker* in San Francisco and Seattle with the great Olympic Champion Robin Cousins playing the Prince. Robin is not only one of the most electrifying performers on the ice today, he's also so much fun to work with. It was a wonderful experience and one I hope to repeat many times. I have done a great deal of television, the latest project being *Romeo and Juliet* which I made with Dwight Hemion and Gary Smith as a special for CBS–TV.

In addition to appearances with Ice Capades, I skate exhibitions at Ice Capades Chalets across the country. I have made a number of appearances as a special guest exhibitor in the new circuit for professional skaters—ProSkate—and have also appeared in Dick Button's annual team championship. Future plans include guest appearances with The John Curry Skating Company. John has established an ice ballet company of his own and I look forward to the opportunity to appear with two of the people I most admire in skating—John and Janet Lynn. I have many dreams still out there on the horizon, but I feel confident that, sooner or later, if I work hard enough, they will all come true.

WHEN I was in Los Angeles to sign my first contract with the Ice Capades in 1976, I received a telephone call from Desi Arnaz, Jr., asking me to dinner. That

Dean

dinner changed my whole life. When Desi arrived to pick me up, Dean Martin, Jr. was with him. I have never asked, but I have a feeling that dinner was really Dean's idea. Shortly after we arrived at the restaurant, Desi saw some friends and went to join them, leaving Dean and me to talk. We have been talking ever since. Five years after that first dinner, we were married in Beverly Hills. Desi was an usher at our wedding.

I think I knew from the moment I met Dean that he was the man for me. But I also knew that he had been married before—to the actress Olivia Hussey, when he was only nineteen years old. I was determined that neither of us would rush into anything. I didn't want us to make a mistake. I may be old-fashioned but I believe that marriage is a lifetime commitment. It is for me, anyway. I also know that a good marriage takes work—it doesn't just happen all by itself. Dean and I both have very busy careers, and we are aware of the threat that can pose to a marriage, so we try to arrange our lives so that we are free at the same time. We like nothing better, when we are home together, than to lock the door, light the candles, pour the wine and spend a quite evening alone.

*Our wedding,
January 8, 1982,
Beverly Hills*

*Below, with Mom, Dad,
Bill and Marcia*

WITH CHANGES in my own life have come changes in my relationship with my family. My mother had not been well at all during the last days of my Olympic preparation, but at the time I was only vaguely aware of it. I thought maybe she was just tired. Then one day during my first year with the Ice Capades I was shocked to receive a cable saying my mother was in the hospital. She had just undergone a radical mastectomy. I flew immediately to visit her and we spent some very close time together. At last I could tell her how much I loved her and needed her and for a week we were able to talk about things we had never taken the time to discuss before. She recovered marvelously, so we were very lucky. These days she and my dad are enjoying the chance to make up for the long years of separation and sacrifice. The simple luxury of being able to spend time together is something they never tire of.

Mom's brush with cancer made me conscious of the nature of life—how precious it is—and of the need for all of us to do what we can to help one another. I decided to take an active role in the American Cancer Society and served as National Youth

Suga

Dorothy Hamill Day, Greenwich, Connecticut, March 21, 1976

Chairman for a year, working at fundraising events and speaking at dinners across the country.

I will never forget the night I was to address the American Cancer Society at their annual dinner in Los Angeles. I have never been a relaxed public speaker. I get very nervous and read from carefully prepared notes. Danny Kaye was the Master of Ceremonies, and I sat beside him all through the dinner, quaking with fright at the prospect of giving a speech before so many people. At last it was time for me to join him at the podium, and as he handed me the microphone, he reached out and took my notes from my hand. I watched him tear my lifeline into shreds. He smiled at my ashen face and said, "That, Ladies and Gentlemen, was Dorothy Hamill's speech. Now she is going to tell you what she really thinks—from her heart." My mind went blank and I began to panic. Danny leaned over to me and whispered, "Just tell them about your mom—the way you told me."

Once the first few words were out of my mouth, I forgot my fear. I found myself telling the story just as Danny told me to. He taught me a valuable lesson that day and I have tried hard to remember it, no matter what I am doing. He taught me that the basis of everything we ever do in our lives has to be sincerity.

WHILE I was putting in eight-hour days training for the Olympics, my brother and sister were working just as hard to reach their professional goals. Sandy, the

With Danny Kaye

My new family

mad chemist of my childhood, became a doctor and Marcia, a
microbiologist. I wasn't surprised about Sandy, but I still marvel
that the sister I thought was a social butterfly is now a scientist,
and one of my closest friends. They are both married and I am
a doting aunt.

There was a time when I wanted a hundred children, but
now I think I will settle for two. In the meantime I do a great
deal of work with children, and whenever I go into a city to
perform I try to arrange to teach an ice skating clinic for the
handicapped. I want to let these special children know how

With a new friend at a March of Dimes skating clinic

important they are and to share with them some of the good fortune I have had in my own life. When I watch them struggling to achieve goals they have set for themselves—small goals for others, giant goals for them—I am always overwhelmed by their courage. When I leave them I take away with me a renewed sense of hope and belief in the essential value of life.

I THINK the greatest sadness in my life since I turned professional is the death of my grandparents. I had wanted so much for them to be around to share everything with me. It was a long time before I stopped thinking, "Oh, I must tell Jonsie about this." They had always been such an integral part of my life.

Bill had been sick for some time when I got married, but I was determined to bring him out to be with me. I hired a nurse and made special arrangements with the air lines. And he was there at the wedding, looking very chic in his blue suit. At the reception he danced with the bride. The following morning Dean and I postponed our honeymoon by a day so that I could spend some time with Bill. I will always be glad I did so, because he died a month later.

Jonsie didn't live to see me marry Dean, but I think she knows about it anyway. When she first met him, not long after we had become engaged, she studied him for a long while and said, "You better look after her, young man. If you don't, I'll come back and haunt you."

The last time I saw her, shortly before she died, I gave her my Olympic medal. "I want you to have this, Jonsie," I said.

She smiled at me through her tears. "Just think, Dorothy, it all started down there on our pond."